Series 6

Explorations of the Green Arte

Volume 1

VIRIDIS GENII: EXPLORATIONS OF THE GREEN ARTE

SERIES 6

VOLUME 1

Edited by Catamara Rosarium,
Marcus McCoy, & Kim Schwenk, MLIS

Viridis Press
2021

Viridis Genii: Explorations of the Green Arte, Volume 1

Note to Readers:

Every precaution possible has been made to verify the contents herein. Any folk remedies mentioned within these pages are for informational purposes only and are not intended to be used as a substitute for medical advice. The publisher, editors and author/s are not responsible and will not be held liable for the results the reader may experience from using any methods mentioned.

Viridis Press
Shelton, WA 98584
USA

viridisgenii.com

Cover Design and Layout by Chris Tiemeyer, Katie Karpetz, & Viridis Press

ISBN – 978-0-578-90804-5
First published by Viridis Press in 2021

Table of Contents

List of Figures and Art

Preface & Foreword

The Viridis Genii Symposium, as well as our previous book series, 'Verdant Gnosis' took pause in our sixth year due to the global pandemic. This was disappointing for us, as well as many, but nothing in comparison to the larger picture we all had to endure, and are still dealing with during these uncertain times. We paused, in bated breath, along with the rest of the world and responded to the global crisis during this unprecedented time the best we could, opting to postpone the event as well as our annual publication. During this time a new shape emerged from the void for the published papers resulting in a new name for our book series, the birth of our publishing imprint, and our 1st ever worldwide Virtual Event.

The natural world is full of dynamic change, death and rebirth. Adaptation, transmutation, and innovation is required in order to deal with those constant challenges we face. And with that, the green genii required us to adapt for the growth of our event and publication, and thus it has taken new form in order to better handle these changes. We are very excited to introduce to you our new publication and press. '*Viridis Genii, Explorations of the Green Arte,* will continue to feature articles written by our esteemed presenters from each symposium and will now be published by Viridis Press.

Our goal is to give an opportunity for teachers, and those that carry wisdom, a place to bring their voice to those who are seeking it. To curate a platform in writing and in space, an opportunity to effect change, to broaden the depth of knowledge for both Herbalists and Esoteric practitioners from around the globe. While at the same time cultivating a cross cultural exchange between traditions working in a medium in which we come together in mutual respect and collaboration.

The birth of The Viridis Genii Symposium in 2015 and past Verdant Gnosis book series has resulted in bringing a tremendous amount of awareness and insight to a community where it was largely before lacking. Where initially there was only a small seed, that small seed has grown into a lush thriving plant that has in turn given seed itself, and those seeds carried and then planted by others. Our vision is being propagated, nurtured and being grown by others in the community near and far. This new incarnation of the book series is an attempt to further distribute the seeds and cuttings of the green spirit which have been cultivated within these pages, the participants, and in the communal gathering that take shape at the event.

These words flow from thought to form on May 1st, 2021, Beltane. The opportunity to write has been sparse these days as we are so very busy during these strange times. In writing this preface we had a chance to reflect upon what drives us to do this work. Clarity. Precious, precious clarity. Clarity of purpose and clear seeing. Clear hearing, clear knowing. It is through our relationship with the plant world that we have found clear vision, clarity of purpose and clarity within self. Sharing that clarity with others and finding those that wish to do the same has been a massive part of our mission with this great work. A great rectification was in order and we are grateful for the pause and changes that allowed this to occur. May these pages and the thoughts therein cultivate clarity and new questions in your explorations of the green arte.

The Viridis Genii is the green spirit, the intelligence and life force that is both hidden and revealed. It is the animating force of the wild wood and the depths of the sea. It shrouds us; it engulfs us with its veiled green mist that awakens the heartbeat that delivers fecundity to the earth, the very essence of life. It is the Green Gnosis one receives from their deep connection and communion with the genus loci.

Deep within these mysteries we find magic, we find myth, we find doorways, pathways, and keys, which allow us to enter the heavens and other worlds as well as guide us through the chthonic realms. We find a great teacher, a master in the arts. We find liberation. We find revelation to the secret workings of the world. It shows us how to create change behind the veil with the aid of those many green beings, which are the body of the green spirit.

We gain wisdom by attending to cycles of the plant world through vine, flower, root, seed, thorn, leaf, and by rod. It is through this gnosis we are shown how to make charms, healing formulas, and where we learn secret teachings and ancient lore of the genii. Each immensely laden with powers and virtues to assist us in blessing and in bane. We make powders, potions, incense, and oils. We make talismans, fetishes, poppets and charms–all with the body of the Viridis Genii.

Through these forces we are given tools to work with to clothe, feed, shelter and heal. It arouses us to lustful frenzy aiding in our lovemaking, the birthing of our children and gives us what we need to protect ourselves. It has helped us share information around the world both ancient teachings and anew. The Viridis Genii gives us everything including our body, as we consume its flesh to make our own.

Blooms and Blessings,
Catamara Rosarium & Marcus McCoy 2021

Introduction

Collectively, the anthology heaves a perpetual sigh of relief, partially from manifesting a sense of survival, but also trusting resiliency, evolution and adaptability of the green spirit that cradles us. The last year has been tragic, disconcerting, and unstable. At the same time, a familiar sprig of leaf, jets through the cement on the sidewalk, reminding humanity of capability. While not necessarily ideal for the Viridis Genii community, technology does support the principals we want to embody by hosting the actual symposium virtually. Regardless, print is still powerful, information is key. This anthology exists as a physical form and a tangible record of the stories and experiences Viridis Genii manages to cultivate. We present eight voices, eight seeds to mature in the information mycelium.

At the beginning of the anthology, the story unfolds with Paul Beyerl, our invited keynote speaker and master herbalist. Paul is contemplative and empathetic, a transcribed thought, sharing a profound narrative of the green spirit teachers and decades of cumulative wisdom. Continuing on, we are invited by Brandon Weston into the Ozark woods and the spiritual, purgative, and emetic rituals of the traditional folk medicine 'Yarb' doctors. We then dig deep with Professor Charles Porterfield, listening to the important work of the Southern hoodoo conjure folk and dispelling misinformation around 'goofer dust'. Next, as mighty as the pen, Richard Spelker confronts traditional magical ink-making formularies with actual applications and personal practical recipes.

The next two authors navigate the plant spirit from home and hearth. Giulia Turolla recollects a beautiful ancestral story from Italy of plant lore and the legacy of family. Similarly, Jesse Hathaway Diaz guides us on a path down to embrace la *Santisima Muerte*; full on with fire and *el corazón*. Lastly, the final authors, Brita Wynn Dinsmore invokes an exploration of cerebral sentience with plants, both spiritually and consciously, while alchemist Robert Bartlett closes the anthology with a metaphysical journey to the center of plant alchemy and the pursuit of Quintessence.

In spite of the difficult current times, the narratives are visceral, self-reflective, and ingenious, as the authors spent moments in their kitchens, gardens, hands covered in dirt with their eyes to the heavens. It seems we are sitting with ancestors and the generational imprints we need to learn. The essence of Viridis Genii is overwhelming, visible, but feral. Overall, allow the words to resonant with you in practice within your physiology and answer the call of the green.

-Kim Schwenk, 2021

The World of Herbal Magic: A Meta-Analysis of Twentieth-Century Ethnobotanical Research

Paul Beyerl

A twenty-first century herbalist who wishes to achieve professional status faces limited choices. There are numerous educational programs available, but there has been no profession oversight as is found in other professions. The American Herbalists Guild [AHG][1] has made remarkable strides in setting standards and providing education which can lead to credentials which have a stellar reputation. Observing the AHG as it evolved over the years, my mind often turned to numerous other professions which organized themselves over the years. Whether the National Funeral Directors Association or the American Medical Association, there are similarities. Were herbalists to follow such a path, there could be a huge social and economic gap dividing those who have those valued credentials and those who do not.

For many millennia, the role of an herbalist was one which encompassed medicine and psychology, religion and magic. Today an herbalist who wishes to be taken seriously faces hundreds upon hundreds of books suitable for the herbalist wishing science-based medicine as a goal. But what of the herbalist who feels a kinship with our heritage when one healed not just the physical, but also the spiritual component of the patient?

---

[1] American Herbalist Guild. Accessed March, 2021.

Routes of Entry

The potential of an herb may enter a practitioner's field via many routes. Not all herbalists aspire to emulate the American Medical Association. Not all herbalists would see themselves wearing white sterile smocks with pockets stuffed with checks from medical insurance companies. There is that herbalist who looks at the jar of bright green leaves comminuted to the perfect size and wonders how to best extract the sesquiterpene lactones and blend them with binders then stuff them into gelatin capsules so the flavor would be completely concealed.

And then there is that herbalist who rubs some of the leaves between her fingers, breathes deep, then closes her eyes and sinks into the scent, letting her inner conscious mind listen for any stories…Recollecting one of these herbalist's thoughts:

> *After a few minutes her eyes opened. She picked up a pencil and began jotting notes onto a large pad of paper.*
>
> *Who were they? Oh, yes…*
>
> *She wrote Fannie and Jeremiah… Robert and Diane… Jessie and Frank…*
>
> *How very odd… I haven't thought about Robert and Diane since…*
>
> *She poured herself a cup of the water extraction of the herb and went to the oriel window where the wood rocking chair waited.*
>
> *A very unpleasant memory tumbled forth. The last time she saw Fannie was at the Cat and Thistle, a pub frequented by many of her friends and where she would always find familiar, friendly faces. Jerm and Fannie both had a little too much to drink. Months of marital tension began to seep out until they were throwing hurtful words at each other. Their friends were stunned. They knew the couple had problems but none of them suspected it to be this bad.*
>
> *Jesse stopped by the shop just the other day. He was bubbling over*

in happiness about the romance that was now weeks old and he could hardly wait to introduce her to this new man in his life...But wait.

She stopped rocking...

What about Frank?

She paused.

She wrote: It has to do with a failed (failing?) relationship...

I believe the majority of us turn not to the most skilled herbalists of any generation, but to the best of herbal historians. This is an exploration of these herbalists who exemplify these top qualities.

Maud Grieve (4 May 1858 - 21 December 1941)

Maud Law was born May 4 in London, 1858. I find no mention of her mother although at the death of her father when she was only six, she was cared for by relatives. When she was 21 her uncle passed away and she inherited £1000. So little is known about her life, yet a sunrise astrological chart for her birth indicates a woman who is intensely private about her own life, but someone with a very strong will and strong convictions.

In 1883, at age 25 we found her in India, now married to William Grieve. William, originally from Edinburgh, was 37 years old at their marriage. Grieve managed the Bally Paper Mill near Calcutta, a position he held for five years prior to their marriage, and which he continued to hold until 1894 when he retired at age 48. The couple returned to England in the early 1900s, trying several homes until 1906 when they settled at Chalfont St. Peter in a house William designed. Maud's domain was the one and half acres of land upon which she created a perennial garden which reflected what her interests must have been during her years in India.

We know that she worked with charities and with a medical mission. World War I mobilized Maud Grieve. She turned her gardens into an herb farm to raise medicinal plants for the war. She founded the National Herb Growing Association in 1914 and became President of the British Guild of Herb Growers (est. 1918). She continued to promote herbal medicines even after the war.

With her work for the war effort done, she wrote more than 300 individual pamphlets or monographs on individual medicinal species. These were edited by Hilda Leyel, NSA *Modern Herbal* was published in 1931. We have a first edition set published by Jonathan Cape, London, here in our research library.

Maud Grieve's knowledge of herbs was tremendous. She was well-educated in botany, as well. With six planets in Taurus (balanced by Mars in Scorpio), she was passionate about her love of herbal medicine. She collected information. When Grieve's monographs reached Hilda Leyel, the modern herbal world was reborn. As Leyel outlines in her introduction:

> *"Botany and medicine came down the ages hand in hand until the seventeenth century; then both arts became scientific, their ways parted, and no new herbals were compiled. The botanical books ignored the medicinal properties of plants and the medical books contained no plant lore. The essence of a herbal was the combination of traditional plant lore, the medicinal properties of the herbs, and their botanical classification. From the time of Dioscorides[2]down to Parkinson in 1629 this herbal tradition was unbroken. Culpeper's popular herbal was discredited with*

---

[2] Grieve, Maude, *A Modern Herbal: The Medicinal, Culinary, Cosmetic and Economic Properties, Cultivation, and Folk-Lore of Herbs, Grasses, Fungi Shrubs & Trees With All Their Modern Uses*, Ed. Mrs. C. F. Leyel. (London: Jonathan Cape, 1931).

scientific people because it was astrological."[3]

Leyel learned of Grieve's work and they met. Leyel took the pamphlets to Mr. Cape who "agreed to publish them if [Leyel] would collate and edit them and see that the American herbs were also included." [4]

In fact, she deserves more recognition. The next name is not on my list due to his work directly, but due to the name recognition. Despite any shortcomings he may have had as an herbalist, this book has endured. I think it would be in the top five on a majority of lists of most famous Herbals. What keeps Grieve at the top of my list is her inclusion of folklore as part of the essential knowledge of a species. It is not included as a curiosity nor to provide humor for the person consulting the book.

John Gerard (c. 1545 - 1612)

Gerard was an English botanist with a large herbal garden in London. His fame today lies in the tradition of the herbal. Gerard's *Herbal* was first published in 1597.

> *"Except for additions of some plants from his own garden and from North America, Gerard's Herbal is largely an unacknowledged English translation of Rember Dodoens's Herbal, published in 1554, itself highly popular in Dutch, Latin, French and other English translations. Gerard's Herball contains profuse, high-quality drawings of plants, with the printer's woodcuts largely derived from Continental European sources, but there is an original title page with a copperplate engraving by William Rogers.Two decades after Gerard's death, the book was corrected*

---

[3] ibid.

[4] ibid

and expanded to about 1700 pages."[5]

Gerard became apprenticed to a barber-surgeon, a man who had a large surgical practice. He did well, moving up over the years. At age 24 he was permitted to open his own practice. He was also known to exaggerate his reputation during his lifetime and the work which has given him lasting fame, the *Great Herball, or, Generall Historie of Plantes* which was published in 1597 and "was considered the best and most exhaustive work of its kind, and a standard reference for some time."[6]

It is certainly a flawed work. The publisher was John Norton, who held the title of "Queen's Printer." Norton "approached Gerard regarding a possible English translation of Dodoens' popular herbal, *Stirpium historiae pemptades sex* (1583)."[7]

Gerard had established his reputation having published his *Catalogue,* "a list of rare plants (1,039 different kinds) he cultivated in his own garden at Holborn." When the *Herball* was published there was material included from previous work by others, often done so in a manner likely "to disguise the original source." The illustrations were from woodblocks which had already been used in one or more earlier botanical books. "Gerard's lack of scientific training and knowledge led him to frequently include material that was incorrect, folklore or mythical."[8] The woodblocks were often mislabeled.

He died in 1612. He was not well educated and was not a botanist, yet "because it was a practical and useful book, packed with helpful drawings of plants, and because he had a

---

[5] John Gerard. Wikipedia. Accessed September, 2019.

[6] ibid.

[7] ibid.

[8] ibid.

fluid and lively writing manner, his *Herball* was popular with ordinary literate people in seventeenth-century England."[9] The lasting popularity of Gerard's work, including its controversy, gives us insight into the manner in which herbals evolved.

Dioscorides (c. 40–90 CE)

Pedanius Dioscorides was a physician in Greece who was the author of *De Materia Medica,* a work in five volumes, which was a standard text for 1500 years. "*De Materia Medica* is the prime historical source of information about the medicines used by the Greeks, Romans, and other cultures of antiquity." It includes plant names from cultures which "otherwise would have been lost." It later states that "*De Materia Medica* formed the core of the European pharmacopeia through the nineteenth century…"[10]

William Crooke (6 August 1848 - 1923)

"This list of the works of William Crooke (1848–1923) represents much of his literary output in pursuit of his interests in ethnology and folklore, for which he was for many years considered to be a leading authority. "In addition to the items listed below in respect of *Folk-lore Record* and its successor, *Folk-lore, the Journal of the Folklore Society,* Crooke also contributed frequently to that journal in the form of letters and brief observations. He was editor of the journal from 1915 until his death. In addition to these works, Crooke made many contributions to the *Encyclopedia of Religion and Ethics*. He had been editing the *Katha Sagara Kosa,* as translated

[9] ibid.

[10] Dioscorides. Wikipedia. Accessed September, 2019.

by Charles Henry Tawney, at the time of his death."[11]

> *"While an administrator in India, he found abundant material for his researches [sic] in the ancient civilizations of the country. He found ample time to write much on the people of India, their religions, beliefs and customs. He held charge as Magistrate and Collector of various districts such as Etah, Saharanpur, Gorakhpur and Mirzapur, and would have held sole power over around 300,000 people with regard to judicial and revenue matters."*[12]

It strikes me as quite within the realm of possibility that Maud could have met William Crooke in India. Crooke would have already been there a decade. They were both interested in the preservation of information, Maud about botany and herbals and herbal folklore. There is nothing which indicates this may have been reality, but Maud and her husband William Grieve were near Calcutta, not an unreasonable trip from the areas under Crooke's administration.

The combination of Maud Grieve and Hilda Leyel produced an herbal which is perhaps the most useful and valued, found among the reference books of almost every herbalist. Certainly, my two-volume copy had a great amount of use. For me *A Modern Herbal* came to represent a line drawn in the pages of herbal history.

My own herbal, *The Master Book of Herbalism,* came into print in 1984. It took only a couple of years, and I discovered that I could not remember the sources for some of the material in the book. I went to my notebooks and notecards and there were those quotes in question but...no source. Well, that was embarrassing. I realized that the lesson my secondary school teacher, Mrs. Margaret Armstrong, tried to teach me was important. Always a good idea to document your source

---

[11] William Crooke. Wikipedia. Accessed September, 2019.

[12] Crooke

material.

I started over with my collection of magical trivia. I went through *A Modern Herbal* line by line by line. I decided that my criteria would be set by Mrs. Grieve. I found that so much modern herbal magic in print had no source material. It would be stated as factual yet it appeared to be the product of the herb's *story* for that individual and at times the author's imagination and wishful thinking. Does that mean it is wrong? No, but I felt there was something not quite right when implying that a property of an herb has stood the test of time when, in fact, it is a concept originating with a contemporary author.

I dedicated myself to the study of documented, academically sound information. When *A Compendium of Herbal Magick* was published I begged and pleaded for my footnotes, but was told that the book would not be published with them. Already a large book, the publisher was not willing to add another 200 pages of notes just to appease an author.

Ethnobotany

"Ethnobotany is the study of how people of a particular culture and region make use of indigenous plants. Ethnobotanists explore how plants are used for such things as food, shelter, medicine, clothing, hunting, and religious ceremonies. Ethnobotany has its roots in botany, the study of plants. Botany, in turn, originated in part from an interest in finding plants to help fight illness."[13] I could go on and on about the books I have added to our library specifically for *this*

[13] Connie Veilleux and Steven R. King, Ph.D., An Introduction to Ethnobotany. Morganstein L., ed. (Shaman Pharmaceuticals, Inc., 1996) http://accessexcellence.org/RC/Ethnobotany/page2.html.

research. There are more than a hundred and twenty, and it pains me to say that a third of them have not yet been combed for magical history.

My specialty is the usage of herbs for religious ceremonies, for folk magic, the use of herbs to change the very image of reality. This is not to imply that I disregard modern science. I spend hours at a time online researching the National Center for Biotechnology Information. Thus, this year my herbal career is 45 years in development. For 45 years I have listened to my peers lamenting the fact that no one studies herbs for their properties. "All of the studies are for the pharmaceutical industry," they moan and we all know the pharmaceutical industry is diabolical.

As a result, we study herbs in so many ways. Scientists globally are looking at the constituents, identifying facets of the herb that slow the growth of cancer, that are useful in the fight against the new potent and frightening bacteria and fungi, and pathogens that are stronger and resistant to the arsenal of antibiotics once useful until we used them so prolifically that we merely helped render them helpless.

While I poke fun at the pharmaceutical industry, the reality is that I have been blessed by them. I would not be alive were it not for their industrious pursuit of fame and fortune. I have lived with HIV for 32 years, I am twice a cancer survivor and, although in my 30s I knew that we should be able to live without anything stronger than herbs, today I recognize that I made the choice to live longer and continue my work. It is a choice only available to me thanks to pharmaceuticals. I believe that a knowledge of herbal chemistry is essential for a thorough knowledge of herbal magic. There are times when those carbohydrates and alkaloids and other compounds which dance around the periodic table are the very building blocks you are manipulating in your ritual work.

The herbs you use should also be studied from the

perspective of herbal horticulture. How does the herb grow? What is its natural growing medium? Write this down: A healthy garden does not need fertilizer. What does the herb do to ensure the survival of its species?

When you are familiar with the shamanic concept which states that to gain control over some entity, some being, you must know its secret name. In other words, if you wished to work with the magic of a particular herb, you should know its secret name. How do you get those names? It's easy. My years of study brought me to that knowledge. The answer is so simple that most don't believe it.

I know your secret. I know your secret name for yourself. This is something I came to understand having conducted numerous past life regressions. What is this great secret I gained without your passcodes? Your secret name is "me." This is the name you use for yourself in almost all of your internal dialogue. We also use "I" but the name "me" is by far the winner.

I once had a wonderful familiar. She answered to the name Elanor. But what was her secret name? It was 'me' in the language she used internally. I knew this because we shared dreams. And in that short time when we both opened our eyes, looking at each other, we spoke the same language.

With that knowledge I took to the gardens. I wished to see if this would hold true—and it does. How could it not? You think your name is so valuable. You sign legal papers and financial payments and leases...But when it comes right down to it, you call yourself 'me' and 'I' just like all species in all languages.

To study an herb means knowing what 'me' is for that herb. Understanding the plant botanically, understanding what biochemicals are created out of the periodic table, knowing the world from that plant's perspective. Unfortunately, we are so arrogant. We define a medicinal herb in terms of what it does for us. But what does the plant do for itself? That is the foundation of that plant's identity. And then there is this: What are its stories?

What is an herb without its soul?

I would say that an herb without its soul would be somewhat superficial. I would like to suggest that the soul of an herb is eminent when it is busy manifesting its sense of 'me.' I further believe that a species has an identifiable character but that there may be individual nuances. If I take a precise dose of *Atropa belladonna* tincture from plants grown in the Puget Sound, I should be able to expect near identical results from *Atropa belladonna* grown in a garden in Dover, U.K. The differences are likely to be subtle enough that the average person would be unable to perceive them. These results may be at the level of biochemistry, a fairly predictable outcome of tropane alkaloids, flavonoids and hydroxycoumarins, among other compounds, interacting with the central nervous system and muscle tissue, but there is more.

I have a long relationship with atropine. In 1973 I was preparing to travel to London for a week of theatre. I was traveling with an oncologist from the Mayo Clinic's main campus in Rochester, Minnesota, where I lived at the time. It was little more than ten years since I had graduated secondary school and been on my own. I had not yet been able to calm the frequent bouts of loose bowels, the result of years of verbal and emotional abuse from my mother. We would be flying nonstop from Chicago O'Hare to Heathrow, in those days a longer flight than today. The odds of urgent and immediate access to a toilet were high, but not within the realm of possibility. The doctor wrote a prescription for tincture of atropine. It worked wonderfully. It is still used today as treatment for some types of diarrhea caused by chemotherapy.

Just two years later, I began a serious journey into the study of herbal medicine. It was another twenty years before I had a small bed of belladonna fully acclimated to our climate and soil. Since then, I spent twenty years experiencing *Atropa belladonna* as a *being*. Not as a *being* as we refer to others of our species, but as a being with her own history and genetic evolution.

The *Atropa belladonna* species has a sense of self. When the plants in our garden produced fruit almost as large as a cherry tomato, filled with that stunning violet juice, there was a sense of pleasure and pride but neither of those words speaks truth for it was a manifestation of the *Atropa* simply being itself, that sense of 'me' for its species, and words borrowed from the human vocabulary coined for humans are woefully inadequate. But I have experienced her soul, soul being a word which is for us but for the *Atropa* would best be her 'inner me.' Several of the growing seasons teaching in our gardens, I worked with a small, but select group of students. After I felt that I had imparted the basic skills and as much knowledge and wisdom as could be done in a classroom, I would then, upon the student's arrival, give them a container with a water extraction (usually an infusion) of one of the 600 species in our private botanical garden, and send them off to the bed or garden where that species was growing.

The student's goal was to bring back information from the plant itself, from the constituents running through the student's body, from the *being* living in our botanical garden. It would only be after a time, thirty minutes or more, that we would gather in the classroom, each student bringing their notes. As the students' skills evolved, more and more they would come back with 'stories' which were surprisingly in line with the known medicinal properties and oftentimes with the folklore and the magical uses. It was the latter which was of particular interest to me. Students in our masters program are expected to learn to identify constituents by flavor, by the taste. It is a skill not unlike that of a well-versed chef, who can identify by taste the ingredients and the seasonings used. But where are the records for the soul of the herbal world? Those stories are the oral tradition. This is material that I search for in this specialized field. Perhaps, recall the herbalist I mentioned at the beginning of my paper? She was letting the herb speak.

Would an ethnobotanist recollect a story like this? No, this might well be a different story. When you are relating one of your stories to a friend, it is significantly different than if you were telling your doctor, or therapist, or parent. It is my belief, which meant it is subject to being wrong, that the first herbalist's story is what we find in books by contemporary authors who write about herbal magic from their own experience and perspective, but independent of research into what their predecessors might have found.

To offer you a story which exemplifies my perspective, let me include two excerpts from some of my favorite stories. These have to do with "the curious question of marriages to trees."[14]

"In some parts of Kangra if a betrothed, but as yet unmarried girl, can succeed in performing the marriage ceremony with the object of her choice round a fire made in the jungle with certain wild plants, her betrothal is annulled and this informal marriage holds good."[15]

> *"In Nepál every Newér girl is, while a child, married to a bel fruit, which after the ceremony is thrown into some sacred river... When she arrives at puberty a husband is selected for her, but should the marriage prove unpleasant, she can divorce herself by the simple process of placing a betel nut under her husband's pillow and walking off."*[16]

---

[14] Crooke, W., An Introduction to the Popular Religion and Folklore of Northern India, (Delhi, Low Price Publications, 2003 reprint of 1894 edition.), 258-261.

[15] ibid.

[16] ibid.

Why do I consider these stories 'academically sound?' They have stood a test of time. The belief that a species will facilitate romance would not survive if it didn't work often enough. If you think it 'works' only because the person *thinks* it will work? Why then is the same belief found in cultures separated by thousands and thousands of miles, or by an ocean, or by the passage of time? There is something about the herb, about its energy…

Money Plant, *Justicia capensis* is "used as a charm to attract customers to a business or as a wash to improve chances of obtaining employment."[17] This sounds like a sentence which comes right out of a book published by a popular metaphysical publisher but, in fact, this is from an academic book published jointly by the University of Natal Press, The University of Zululand and the National Botanical Institute. This is a story which has survived in the Zulu culture and when research was done, the source was documented by A. B. Cunningham, a researcher known in South Africa.

This takes me to a second criteria. That magical story about the usage of Money Plant may be just a sentence sounding like a modern spellbook, but it is a belief which is not held by one person, but by (at least) one region where the Zulu peoples lived. That book is one for which I have my own story. I ordered it from South Africa online. Imagine my shock and joy when I found the book to be "number 14 of a limited edition of 300 copies." The book has since been reprinted and marketed as a softbound book. How did I find that book? Although I joke that the skill of water dowsing I had as a child now finds me books online, there is a more truthful answer.

---

[17] Hutchinson, Anne. compiler. Zulu Medicinal Plants.(Natal, South Africa: South Africa Press, 1996), 291.

I became a member of the American Botanical Council in 2002. It took several years of purchasing books from their catalog. And what books! These were books an herbalist would only dream of and, back then, it was nearly impossible to know they existed. One book I purchased, not knowing what I was getting, was *Native American Ethnobotany* by Daniel Moerman.

Moerman[18] is an anthropologist who spent 25 years gathering this information. All types of usage, including ceremonial and folk magic, on more than four *thousand* plant species. If only every continent, every region could have such a book. It took me more than two years, but I went through the information on each species line by line. Because of this, I learned to value the field of ethnobotany and I find nuggets of pure gold.

I was teaching an intensive at Ceratonia Gardens in Portugal and wished to demonstrate the website. I typed in the title of one of the books which shaped my life as Priest and as herbalist. *Occult Science In Medicine...*What did I find? A bookstore in London had a first edition of the book published in 1893. I placed my order before anyone else could come along. Many times I enter a few key words and see what comes up. Then I look for titles which suggest promise.

India continued the process begun during the British occupation. Maude Grieve and William Crooke were not alone in their interests. Decades earlier Charles Darwin set a high standard as a British naturalist. At its strength, the British Empire covered a quarter of all land on our planet and a quarter of all people. For someone who can read only one language, English provides me with access to vast amounts of information. The timing of the dominance of Britain and then the United States and the arrival of the internet bring us many books from countries who have their own language, written in

---

[18] Moorman, Daniel E. Native American Ethnobotany.

English for the tourist and the international market.

My own research library has books which specialize in the herbs of West Africa, Greece, Tibet, Amazon, India, Himalayas, Caribbean, Scotland, China, Southern Africa, Nepal, Australia, Japan, Philippines and, of course, Europe and the United States. There remain many areas of the world which are not represented. There is another, compelling reason for us to work at having a protected esoteric library: there is a dangerous rise in fundamentalism. The Mafia, in the late 19th and earlier 20th centuries had codes of conduct. Innocent bystanders were not killed. The gangs of today have no problem killing innocent people. In 1961, T. C. Schelling coined the phrase "collateral damage." Thus, we live in an era of terrorism.

In addition, through the mishandling of our precious planet, we face the possibility of the loss of many of our plant species as many are trapped by rising ocean levels and others cannot adapt as fast as necessary. Let me be honest, my sympathies lie with the plant world. Much is being done to save seeds.

"There are about 6 million accessions, or samples of a particular population, stored as seeds in about 13,010 gene banks throughout the world as of 2006. This amount represents a small fraction of the world's biodiversity, and many regions of the world have not been fully explored."[19] Therefore, I am a strong supporter of seed banks. They can help to preserve corporal bodies of the plants being preserved.

Another example of this is in October, 2003, a 'storybooth'[20] was opened in Grand Central Terminal, New York. A story is broadcast weekly on Public Radio. During these years over a quarter of a million individuals have recorded their stories. These are stories about dreams and fear,

---

[19] Seed Bank

[20] StoryCorps. https://storycorps.org/discover

stories of pain, stories so personal that we hear people baring their souls. These stories are protected in the FolkLife Center of the Library of Congress. Which leads me to the question, why cannot we have this for our herbal world? I am not saving the actual stories.

While, I do not have the skills with which to sit with *Crassula orbicularis* in order to determine how and why it shares the same relationship with lightning as does *Sempervivum tectorum*... And just how closely are those two related? What I do have are the stories collected by skilled ethnobotanists, stories based upon *their* experience. Based upon the source materials I've seen authors use, and some of the books which I have dowsed, it is a reasonable claim I make. There are more than 2,100 species for which I have magical information, all from documented sources.

The classification system I initiated for the *Compendium* remained in use as a means of identifying some generalized information about the type of energy or qualities of the species and then, my favorites, one document, now twenty-four pages long, lists deities 'Abellia through Zoroaster' and the species which share history with them, and a different document now thirty-nine pages long which lists the usages by specific topic.

acceptance...amethyst...anointing to Windway
Ceremony...World Card...worries (to dispel)
battle protection...bird magic...business success to
truthfulness...unwanted people (removes)...visualization

It is wonderful material; it is breath-taking to have such a global view of plant magic and of the stories which await us. I doubt this research will be complete in my lifetime. This project, the work I have done and the research library, are now housed on our new eleven-acre Center in the western end of the Driftless Area (a region of 24,000 square miles which was missed by the drift of the last two glaciers).

In closing, I would like to share with you one of the more interesting findings. When I poured through the Daniel Moerman book, I found something I had not seen in other cultures: a myriad of references in which plants were part of magical work to improve one's lot at gambling. It was not uncommon for tribes to meet in order to play lacrosse or have horse races. Gambling was part of the First People's culture to an extent which I do not recall finding elsewhere. Then the invasion of Europeans came in and took away their land. How are they making money today? Casinos. Gambling. I think it is evident from the stories I've shared; I love this work.

Cleanin' the Blood: Ritual Emetics and Purgatives in Ozark Folk Healing

Brandon Weston

Botanical and mineral purgatives serve as a key part of the Ozark folk healing tradition in not only providing a way for individuals to cleanse, or *purge*, out substances seen as poisonous or harmful, but also as one of many methods of spiritual purification. The ritualistic uses of purgatives seek to draw out spiritual entities or influences caught inside the flesh of the human body. This magical poison or *pizen*, as it is sometimes called, is ingested in many ways, but namely through remote cursing or through physical contact[1] with certain *poisoned* ingredients. Purgation is only one of many methods in the category of purification of the body. These ritual acts, as a whole, seek to realign the physical and spiritual body with the world outside. Such works of purification might include washing the body in a river, *smoking* or fumigating a person's body with cleansing plants, or *yarbs*, like red cedar (*Juniperus virginiana*), as well as by forcing out certain bodily fluids through methods like bleeding, cupping, enemas, laxatives, and emetics. While the methods of purification might be diverse, the underlying theory is based on the common idea of returning a person's

[1] Most commonly by eating or drinking.

body, both physical and spiritual, back to a state of equilibrium.

What we might call *physical* purgation includes methods to remove physical_disease or disease-causing agents from the body by using botanical and mineral compounds. In the Ozarks, this job would have originally been held by the specialized *Yarb Doctor,* an individual skilled in the medicinal uses of plants and minerals. These doctors were passed a significant amount of knowledge about plant uses from both European and Indigenous sources. The Yarb Doctor was the first line of defense against physical illness for Ozark hillfolk and although they were often illiterate, many mountain herbalists carried hundreds of individual plant species in their memory. Entering the early twentieth century, availability of access to the local pharmacist and country doctor increased greatly, allowing for commercial compounds like castor oil or ipecac syrup[2] to be introduced into the cabin home as laxatives and emetics. Even with the availability of a local pharmacist, many hillfolk still relied upon their Yarb Doctors to provide their medical care. Even in rural communities today, remedies coming from the earth are believed to be vastly superior to those of *city folk* and shifty medical professionals.

The theory of physical illness in Ozark folk medicine is based upon a simplified humoral theory brought with hillfolk from Europe. Conditions of the digestive system were at one time seen as being of the utmost importance as it was often thought that the general state of a person's health could be determined by a person's digestion. Under the system of the four humors, the digestive system is ruled by the organ liver, the fluid blood, and the season spring. Symptoms of a *sanguine* condition include constipation, diarrhea, bloating, and general poor digestion. Blood then becomes a very important bodily fluid when talking about purgation for the

[2] Derived from the roots of the South American *Carapichea ipecacuanha* tree.

overall health of the body. Protecting the blood from becoming *poisoned* or diseased was then of the utmost importance for the individual. *A Physician in the House, for Family and Individual Consultation,* originally published in 1897 and found in my own Ozark family's home library says, "Constipation, indigestion, impure atmospheric surroundings, improper or insufficient food and mental difficulties may be possible causes of disease of the blood."[3] We can link this theory to the important concept of *cleanin' the blood,* especially in the springtime. Other phrases like, *clearin' the blood, cleanin' the blood,* as well as a third, *blood purifier,* strictly refer to purgative medicines used to treat poor digestion and the *sanguine* condition by removing toxins from the liver and blood itself.

By removing these toxins through purging, the body can return to a state of equilibrium and good health. Practical uses of regular purging are lost upon us in the modern world, unless you participate in *fasting* or *cleansing* culture. Up until the mid-twentieth century much of the Ozarks was still heavily forested and dotted with communities completely isolated from city amenities.

Running water, electricity, and access to proper medical care were distant luxuries to hillfolk. Many people suffered from malnourishment and constant infestation of bodily parasites. Purgatives then became a staple part of life. Strong laxative plants like mayapple (*Podophyllum peltatum*) and senna (*Senna alexandrina*), and mineral compounds like Epsom salts (magnesium sulfate[4]) or castor oil, were used as *vermifuges* to kill and expel internal parasites like tapeworms. Spring tonics and decoctions of yarbs like sassafras (*Sassafras*

---

[3] J.H. Greer, *A Physician in the House, for Family and Individual Consultation*, (Chicago, IL: The Model Publishing Co., 1960) 706.

[4] A naturally occurring mineral throughout the Ozarks. Was often obtained from the local pharmacy.

albidum) and wild cherry bark (*Prunus serotina*) were taken liberally by hillfolk for their mild laxative and fluid dispelling properties. Spring was often seen as a time of personal rebirth and renewal after a winter spent indoors eating canned vegetables and salted meat. Digestion for the average person was likely in its poorest condition at this time of the year, subsequently, blood tonics become an important part of the yearly ritual. Again, Greer's manual says, "In nearly all chronic diseases great benefit will be experienced by an occasional emetic..."[5] Even diarrhea was often cured by a good and strong vomiting. I'll include here Greer's recipe for a simple emetic to be used in almost all cases of blood and liver purification:

Composition Powder:

Bayberry[6] Bark – 1 lb.

Hemlock[7] Bark – ½ lb.

Ginger[8] – ½ lb.

Cayenne[9] – 1 oz.

Cloves[10] – 1 oz.

Pulverize and mix thoroughly. Add one tablespoon of the above *Composition Powder* to one-pint water. Make a strong infusion. Also make an infusion of one teaspoonful of lobelia[11] to one-cup of water. Let cool. The patient should be sat in a

[5] Greer, *A Physician*, 716.

[6] Myrica spp.

[7] Tsuga spp.

[8] Zingiber officinale

[9] Capsicum annum

[10] Syzygium aromaticum

[11] Lobelia inflata, also called *Indian Tobacco*

room where the temperature is, "...comfortable, and at the same time plenty of fresh air should be provided."[12] The patient drinks a half-cupful of the infusion every fifteen minutes until the, "...whole system feels thoroughly warm." At this point, give the patient the lobelia infusion to drink. Vomiting should be avoided immediately for, "...the longer it is delayed the more thoroughly the tissues will be relaxed and the more beneficial will be the results."[13] If vomiting doesn't occur after ten minutes, give more of the *Composition Powder* infusion until catharsis takes place, but no more lobelia.

Greer's recipe would have been beneficial for those with access to a pharmacy and the botanical ingredients he uses, none of which are native to the Ozarks save for lobelia. For the average family living in the isolated hills and hollers, the land itself would need to provide any medicines required. Such plants were known for their ability to *clean, clear, thin,* and *purify* the blood as well as aiding in the treatment of certain specific folk illnesses like a *slow liver,* characterized by bowel and circulation problems. I've divided these medicinal plants as the hillfolk would have, into categories defined by how fast they'll make you run to the outhouse. The first level is called, *Alright, I Can Handle That,* which includes common spring tonics and gentle laxatives like sassafras, wild cherry bark, and slippery elm bark (*Ulmus rubra*), as well as diuretics[14] in the form of dandelion root (*Taraxacum spp.*), burdock root (*Arctium spp.*), and the rare but always popular Solomon's Seal root (*Polygonatum multiflorum.*) Another plant, pokeweed (*Phytolacca americana*) can be included under this heading. The plant itself contains powerful toxins that one normally wouldn't want to consume. The young leaves and

---

[12] Greer, *A Physician*, 717.

[13] Greer, *A Physician*, 717.

[14] Also seen as purgatives because of their action of expelling fluids from the body.

stalks are collected in the springtime and boiled, usually in two or three changings of water, then strained and cooked in a skillet. A low amount of the toxic chemical compounds remains through the cooking process and results in a leafy green that is high in iron and acts as a mild laxative. Apart from pokeweed, tonic plants for digestion are most often made into decoctions, meaning the plant material is left to boil in water for a given amount of time before straining and drinking. Spring tonics are often taken very strongly, but for only a short amount of time, usually one or two cups a day for a week.

The next category is called, *Ok, Now I'm Feelin' Somethin'*, and includes plants known to really *get the body movin'*, as they say. The commercial laxative called *black draught* was famous enough for Dolly Parton to write a song about its curative qualities. It's a semi-strong laxative deriving benefit from the senna plant. My own grandpa tells stories of being frequently *cleaned out* by the medicine as a child. Other laxative plants of this category include flaxseed (*Linum usitatissimum*), butternut bark (*Juglans cinerea*), peach bark[15] (Prunus persica), and Epsom salts. We can also add in a common emetic, Indian tobacco, also called *pukeweed*. Vomiting and shitting often go hand-in-hand as powerfully purifying actions. Both are credited for expelling toxins from the body, although emetics are often employed over laxatives for more serious illnesses.

The last grouping is called, *Oh Good Lord*, and includes plants and minerals known for their quick and often violent action upon the stomach and bowels. Strong laxatives include botanical ingredients like mayapple roots and pawpaw fruit (*Asimina triloba*), as well as pharmaceutical products like

---

[15] The peach tree, as well as other barks like black gum, comes with its own harvesting ritual. It's widely known that cutting the bark in an upwards direction will make a person vomit and cutting downwards will act as a strong laxative.

castor and mineral oils. Emetics and violent purging agents include ipecac syrup, the native black physic root (*Veronicastrum virginicum*) also called Culver's root, black gum bark (*Nyssa sylvatica*), or tobacco (*Nicotiana tobacum*), preferably *wild tobacco* (*Nicotiana rustica*) which has a much higher nicotine content and has had connections to ritual purging for centuries amongst the indigenous peoples of the Americas.

Use of purging plants for physical illness was based entirely upon what might be on hand in the cabin, on the land, or what could be bought quickly from the local pharmacist. Black draught was usually always kept around for use as an effective laxative and every hill family knew to drink sassafras tea in the springtime. Yarb Doctors might start first with a low-level botanical formula then increasing the strength of the brew if the illness persists. Then you have certain doctors who know that "strong medicine forces sickness down and out," as one old timer told me, and "if you ain't throwin' up, it ain't workin'." This might be viewed as counterintuitive to healing, but in Ozark folk belief illness is above all else seen as being caused by a buildup of harmful toxins within the body, specifically in the blood and the liver. By purging frequently, these toxins can be released, and the individual returned to a state of equilibrium.

Spiritual or *magical* purgation is administered in cases of illnesses deemed to have an origin in witchcraft. Diagnosis of such illnesses occurs in many ways, but most commonly a healer determines such cases after all other means of physical healing have been tried to no avail. Exhausting other remedies, the folk doctor then turns to methods of magical diagnosis or recommends the patient go to a doctor who specializes in such work. Not all mountain healers make use of magical remedies and techniques. The Yarb Doctor is almost strictly a folk herbalist, although they often know a few prayers or charms to heighten the effectiveness of their medicinal preparations. Magical cures are the domain of the *Power Doctor* and *Goomer Doctor*. Some might equate these individuals with witches, but there's a firm separation in Ozark belief between those who heal (doctors) and those who hurt (witches.) While many still look at a Power Doctor with suspicion, they'd never dare call them a witch. Healing talent or ability is ultimately seen as a *gift* from a divine power. Power Doctors are consulted only when other cures fail. Using their divinatory techniques, these healers can determine whether an illness is indeed caused by a magical source and how the harm might be remedied and reversed.

As with physical contagion, folk illnesses often have their own names, symptoms, and common remedies. These include illnesses like the *evil eye,* caused by the gaze of a jealous person, usually toward particularly adorable children. The evil eye can manifest as a strong fever that won't break or a rash on the skin in order to magically *deform* the child. Cures for such a *cuss*[16] usually involve a quick response like crossing one's fingers over the child or turning the child's clothes inside out immediately. Other folk illnesses of a magical nature include such mysteries as being *spellt* or *spelled,* another word for being cursed by malign witchcraft, and a similar condition known as *goomering*. The origin of the word is unknown but has given rise to a form of folk healer called the Goomer Doctor who specializes in removing witchcraft off a person. Perhaps the deadliest of the magical illnesses is being infected by *live things*. These include small reptiles, amphibians, and insects that are thought to inhabit the body of the victim and cause a great deal of pain and annoyance.

---

[16] Ozark folk word for a curse, usually brought upon by a certain quick action like the hearing of an owl as an omen for death or dropping of a dishtowel which foretells a quarrel in the home. *Taking off the cuss*, usually involves a quick response as a preventative for any harm, such as throwing salt on the fire when you hear an owl screech or tying a knot in a dropped towel.

Live things I've encountered include small snakes, lizards, frogs, toads, salamanders,[17] worms, cockroaches, wasps, flies, and spiders. The origin of this illness likely has a connection to the real-world effects of internal parasites. The symptoms of both the physical and magical illnesses are often similar and include wasting away, pale color, internal cramping especially in the bowels, and digestive issues. In Ozark belief, these two illnesses aren't linked at all. Worms are easily diagnosed by mountain doctors and cured with vermifuges like wormwood or mayapple. *Live things* are considered a very specific illness, distinguished from other internal parasites by one common symptom; the sensation of crawling things underneath the skin. This alone could drive anyone insane, but coupled with wasting, it's no wonder that hillfolk often seek divine aid and drastic remedies. Catching *live things* is an easier process than one might imagine. A person need only deposit a certain cursed ingredient in their victim's drink or food. This *materia magica* most often includes dried and powdered pieces of the animal themselves. For example, powdered snakeskin for a snake, lizard claws for a lizard, spider eggs for a spider, and so on. Once a person consumes these cursed items[18] they grow and multiply in their body forming *live things*. Some say this happens immediately, others that it'll happen in a certain number of days, usually based on culturally significant numbers like three, seven, twelve, or the unlucky thirteen. *Live things* can only be removed from the body through purgation using emetics. It's best to keep oneself safe by avoiding eating or drinking anything from someone you don't trust.

---

[17] Also called *ground puppies*.

[18] The consensus amongst believers in *live things* that I've met is that just consuming the parts won't make you sick, it's the curse on the items that does damage. "Otherwise, I'd damn near always be sick with all the spiders in this cabin," as one informant told me.

A common method of purifying the body of a magical illness is by purgation, much in the same way one might purge out a physical illness. Methods of purging were taken as seriously by the Power Doctor as any other healer would take their purges of ordinary sickness. The level of the purge, ingredients, and ritual to use were determined by the healer based upon a magical diagnosis, often through dreaming, reading of cards or tea leaves, use of a pendulum or dowsing rods, or the always popular smoke method whereby a healer would drop some tobacco on a lit coal and examine the movement of the smoke trail to determine the illness and direction of origin.[19] After a diagnosis is made, the healer then seeks to determine not only the correct ingredients for the remedy and ritual, but also the proper day and time to enact the purge. In general, considerations of the zodiac, moon sign, and time of day are an important factor in Ozark folk medicine. The *Zodiac Man*, or *Man of Signs* is almost always consulted when determining the proper day to hold a healing session. In this theory, every part of the human body is assigned one of the signs of the zodiac starting with Aries at the head and Pisces at the feet. Healing is only performed when the daily moon sign is in the *opposite* zodiac sign to where the illness or complaint is currently sitting. For example, a headache is in the head, ruled by Aries, so then healing should be performed when the moon is in Libra. Most folk doctors would never wait so long to heal something as simple as a headache or other minor ailments, but the Zodiac Man would certainly be consulted before any *major* healing, such as a ritual to remove a curse from the body or the healing of illnesses like cancer.

The level of purge required is based entirely upon the nature of the magical illness itself. As with physical purges,

---

[19] This is particularly useful in work that will send the illness or curse back to the witch who originally sent it in the first place.

I've divided these levels into several unique categories. The first is called, *Mother-in-Law Looked at Me Sideways,* and encompasses folk illnesses like the evil eye, fear, and other low-level curses thrown onto a person or sent to them by individuals like the mother-in-law who is no doubt a witch but not a very powerful one. This method of purgation employs certain gentle laxatives and diuretics like sassafras root, Solomon's seal root, dandelion root, burdock root, flaxseed, or slippery elm bark. The idea is to help clean out the system, but not to make the person feel uncomfortable. You will no doubt notice that at this level, there is no catharsis by vomiting. In general, this lower level of magical illness doesn't require a physical purge and it's often believed that simply drinking a strong tonic will do the trick.

As in all cases of purging for spiritual purification, the herbal medicines are always paired with *"going to water,"* as it's often called. Ritualistic washing in a moving body of water is a form of purification well ingrained within Ozark culture from many different cultures. These include ancient pagan beliefs from across Europe that value the healing powers of certain springs or wells, as well as a harkening back to the Christian ritual of baptism. There is also a significant influence upon Ozark water beliefs coming from the indigenous peoples of the Southeast[20], especially the Cherokee. Most healers who deal with any of the magical illnesses will always have a proper body of running water in mind for use. The most auspicious would be a river or creek that flows into the west, generally considered the direction of evil and location of the *land of sickness.* Any river will do in a pinch, as long as it has enough moving water to fully submerge the patient. For minor illnesses of a magical origin, a patient might be taken to

---

[20] See Alan Edwin Kilpatrick, "'Going to Water': A Structural Analysis of Cherokee Purification Rituals," *American Indian Culture and Research Journal,* 15.4 (1991): 49-58.

a river before dawn,[21] given a decoction of cleansing plants to drink, then taken into the water, oriented so that they are facing with the current, so as to allow the magical illness to be swept away from the patient, and then physically washed by the healer. After washing, the patient is sometimes given more of the herbal decoction to drink, then allowed to dry off and taken back home.

While simple in nature, this rite represents a powerful form of catharsis and purification. Washing is crucial to the healing process, but is often replaced by a specialized bath when no river is available. In this case, certain healing plants are soaked in a container of water. Spring water is preferred, the most powerful being water collected from inside a cave as it has never seen the light of the sun or moon. This water is most commonly collected in a big iced tea pitcher then covered with a towel to block the light of day. Plants are chosen for their cleansing and protective qualities and most often include red cedar and tobacco, as well as often more specialized yarbs like horsemint (*Monarda spp.*) used for its ability to detach ghosts who cling to a mortal victim, or the widely dreaded asafetida (*Ferula assa-foetida*) whose noxious odor is used to scare away illness and evil. Once chosen, these plants are left to soak in the collected water, usually overnight. The bath is then poured over the patient's head three times, accompanied by prayers or verbal charms. For many healers, while the bath is a good way of cleansing off minor illnesses like evil eye or fear, a river is always preferred if available for its powerfully purifying quality.

The next category is called, *"Widder Looked at Me Sideways,"* and is generally considered to hold illnesses and cursed conditions of a little more serious or urgent nature. The patient might have a prolonged fever that won't break, or a

---

[21] An important time in Ozark folk healing representing cleansing, renewal, and rejuvenation.

general state of wasting away, defined by pale skin and significant weight loss. The *widder* or widow of the community is always looked at with great suspicion. Everyone knows that without a man to keep her in check she's bound to have sold her soul to Satan himself in exchange for magical knowledge, or so the unfortunate tale goes. As with all the levels of magical illness, the patient is first taken to a river or creek before dawn. Next, the patient drinks a purging liquid, usually a simple infusion of lobelia, but is sometimes mixed with other emetic plants like Culver's root or black gum bark. These riverside purges are almost always based in emetics rather than laxatives. The purging drink is then followed by a large amount of a herbal infusion brought to room temperature.

This infusion might include plants to help cushion the stomach and ease the process of purgation. Yarbs include sassafras, mountain mint (*Pycnanthemum spp.*), horsemint, spicebush (*Lindera benzoin*), catnip (*Nepeta cataria*), or German chamomile (*Matricaria chamomilla*). The patient then strips and is taken by the healer into the river where they will then wash or dunk their patient, usually three, seven, or twelve times, accompanied by prayers, verbal charms, and sometimes songs. Occasionally a healer might include a bowl of fresh, crushed plants like sassafras or spicebush leaves that they will mix with water and rub onto the patient's body. While the patient is being washed, they are allowed to purge themselves into the river. A healer will often keep a jug of clean water tied to their back to give to the patient to drink so that the purge will continue.

After the purging and washing ceremony has ended, the patient is taken out of the river, given more of the cushioning infusion to help settle their stomach, then dries, clothes themselves, and returns home. The higher levels of magical illness are almost always accompanied by additional steps that the patient will need to enact in the coming days. In this case, the healer might give the patient a small bag of yarbs and instruct them to go home and brew up a pinch of the powder in a pitcher of water then pour it over their head three times. This ritual bath can be a one-time order, or might continue for the next three, seven, or even twelve days. Another ritual sometimes added at this level is changing the patient's clothes. While at the riverside, the healer will clothe their patient in a new set of garbs then take their old items, still infected with the magical illness, back home to boil in a magical broth. Clothes are also sometimes buried for a given number of days, the idea being the earth will cleanse out the curse or magical illness.

The deadliest category of magical illness falls under the heading, *Oh No, I Done Went and Ate at a Widder's Table,* and is where we find the appearance of *live things.* This illness is identified by certain characteristics specific to *live things* alone, namely the sensation of small creatures crawling underneath your skin. There are also other physical signs that are identified as symptoms of *live things,* including serpentine rashes on the skin and the appearance of numerous bumps or boils.[22] Wasting will almost always be another symptom, as will insanity[23] or the feeling of restlessness. The method for removing *live things* from the body involves a lengthier process, but one that still incorporates common rituals from the other levels. The patient is first brought to the healer's home. This is a rarity as most mountain doctors choose to work in their patient's houses, to keep them calm and relaxed, a vital part of the healing process.

---

[22] Said to be places where the *live things* are attempting to escape from the body.

[23] In the old days, many mental health issues were taken as signs of magical illness and treated with strong purgatives. When I did my tour of the Ozark Mountains collecting folklore, remedies, and recipes, many of the healers I talked to addressed this very issue saying they always send a patient to a doctor in town before ever seeing them. Of course, this may well have been just to placate my questioning.

The healer's home is often thought to be sacred or protected ground. There are many folktales about hillfolk, particularly children, wandering unknowingly onto some mountain wizard's property and receiving quite a fright from their home defenses. It's not a place anyone would willingly go to, not unless they had something seriously wrong with them. The old tales are clear on this, for most magical illnesses the right doctor will always just *appear* at the exact right time, with a big bag of medicines and potions. Sometimes they'll sleep in your cabin with you until the healing is done, other times they'll drop by mysteriously to check in on your progress.

But for those serious illnesses like *live things*, you've got to leave home and seek out someone who *knows things*. These sorts almost always live in isolated places in the woods, underneath big bluffs, or hidden away in some deep, labyrinthine cavern. By seeking out their aid, a patient becomes an active participant in their own healing process. Once in the healer's home, the work begins immediately. The patient is almost always stripped of their old clothes, which are later burned, then given something special to wear for the duration of the ritual. One healer I met always kept around some long-johns and a few flannel shirts just in case a patient stayed over. Even this act is a part of the healing process. The patient sheds their old skin and dons a new set of ritual garbs intended for this one purpose.

They have now exited the land of their birth and have entered into that magical *otherworld*. The patient is then given a tonic, usually made from a strong decoction of sassafras roots mixed with horsemint flowers and spicebush twigs. The healer will make a large amount of this tea as it will serve to help fortify their patient's body before and after the purge. A patient who is purging will almost always be given a large amount of liquid to drink, including the herbal decoction and pure water. Once full up on liquids, the patient is taken to a dark room. Darkness is required for this work, or so I've been told. They're usually situated on a low stool and positioned so that a deep bucket or washbasin could be placed at their feet. The bare-bones ritual for this particular purge is drinking the preliminary herbal tea, going into a dark room, then drinking a purging liquid, and finally throwing your guts up into a bucket. The nuances of the ritual vary from healer to healer, with some including lengthy songs and prayers to be recited or sung over the patient throughout the entire purge, and others might bring in certain ritual objects like rattles, feather brushes, or bundles of herbs used to magically sweep off the illness as it is purged. A strong purging liquid is a recipe that healers will always guard closely. The idea being that if a witch finds out what goes into your special purging potion, they can magically alter the ingredients to render them ineffective or even poisonous to the patient. Most purges at this level will include strong emetics like mayapple, tobacco juice, ipecac syrup, or strongly brewed decoctions of lobelia.

All of these will result in an almost immediate purge. At this point in the ritual, the healer will usually light a candle and give their patient a little water or herbal tea to settle their stomach and allow them to purge again if necessary. Then they will also almost always show their patient the *live things* that have been purged into the bucket. I've sat in on a few of these rituals and in all cases the bucket has contained live animals in addition to vomit. In one case it was three or four young garter snakes, in another it was cockroaches and a large number of dead flies. Seeing these *live things* always evokes a very visceral response in the patient and additional purges.

The debate continues as to whether this is some trick or sleight of hand on the part of the healer. From my own perspective, I've watched healers as closely as I could and have never been able to catch them slipping anything in the bucket, let alone entire live animals. After the purging has subsided, the healer then gives the patient more of the herbal decoction to help settle their stomach and fortify their bodily systems. They are then fed a bland food, usually oatmeal or corn mush. Once they can keep the food down, the work moves past purgation. Often a healer will insert a specialized ritual here. The patient is blindfolded, taken outside, and buried in a shallow grave with only their face left out.

They are then watched over by the healer for a given amount of time, usually from dusk to dawn. The next morning, before sunrise, the patient is either dug out of the ground, or woken up if there was no burial involved in the healing rites, then taken by the healer out to a river. As in the other levels of purging, the patient is stripped bare and washed, always facing in the direction of the current, in order to watch their illness be carried away.

They are then given new clothes to wear and taken back home. In the direst of cases, the patient might be given a new name by the healer and a fresh baptism. Almost as important as the purge itself are the daily baths using specific blends of magical plants that the patient is instructed to take. These baths usually last for at least twelve days, but could go for as long as a month. The patient's condition is reassessed by the healer at the end of this period and it is determined whether or not to start the entire ritual process anew.

Ritual purging is only one of many works of magical purification in the Ozarks but is often said to be the most powerful. Whether or not actual animals are drawn out of the body in cases of *live things,* is beside the point. The physical and mental affect such catharsis has upon a sick patient, who hasn't found relief from any other medical practitioner, cannot be ignored. Beyond being just a *psychosomatic* or placebo remedy, the fact remains that in many cases these purging rituals work and without leaving long-lasting side effects for the patient.

Such magical purges have developed across the world from within cultures whose medical system is based on what was on hand, what could be gathered, and what could be repurposed. Purging rituals exist because there has been a need for such visceral catharsis in order to heal illness with no known physical cause. These illnesses didn't go away with the availability of modern medicine and affordable healthcare. In the Ozarks, still to this day, there are healers who use purging, whether by laxatives or emetics, in their healing work much to the benefit of their patients. There is some primal part of our human nature that still seeks out these medicines to cleanse us of spiritual illness and reconnect us to the most basic processes of our own bodies.

References:

Cavender, Anthony. *Folk Medicine in Southern Appalachia.* Chapel Hill, NC: The University of North Carolina Press, 2003.

Randolph, Vance. *Ozark Magic and Folklore.* New York, NY: Dover Publication, 1964.

Kilpatrick, Alan Edwin, "'Going to Water': A Structural Analysis of Cherokee Purification Rituals," *American Indian Culture and Research Journal,* 15.4 (1991): 49-58.

Greer, J.H. *A Physician in the House, for Family and Individual Consultation.* Chicago, IL: The Model Publishing Co., 1960.

Storl, Wolf D. *The Untold History of Healing.* Berkeley, CA: North Atlantic Books, 2017.

Goofer Dust: The History, Substance, and Use of the 'Killing Powder' of Southern Conjure

Professor Charles Porterfield

Within the tradition of hoodoo and Southern conjure, there is a fair amount of cursing and 'killing work' that is done directly by or on behalf of clients or workers. One hears tales of 'graveyard work,' 'putting sickness' in someone, of 'taking someone to the cemetery,' and terrifying tales of people having living creatures take up residence inside their bodies because someone has put 'live things' in them. Amongst all this, though, one particular method stands out head and shoulders above all the rest - the compounding and use of the lethal Goofer Dust.

Also known as Goober or Gopher Dust or Powder, it is sung about in song, regaled in story, and whispered about by those fearing it. Goofer Dust is a vital, if not mysterious, part of hoodoo and Southern conjure, but just what is this baleful powder so well known for killing and harming? Where did it originate, how is it made, and how is it used? Perhaps most importantly we must also ask 'why has it survived?' this 'hurting powder,' this 'killing dust,' and how has it come to be regarded by many as a purely spiritual product when once it was known to be 'pure poison' and handled with inordinate care and concern?

The best place for us to start our exploration of this most notorious of all hoodoo formulas is to first understand that Goofer Dust is, in fact and origin, poison! Not a euphemistic or oblique 'poison,' but a literal biological substance capable of causing physical and mental damage or even death. This legacy of being poisonous finds it way even into the language which surrounds Goofer Dust – one 'poisons' a victim with it or 'is poisoning them;' the victim of being 'goofered' has been 'hurt.' As the tradition moved away from its African roots and the more toxic version of Goofer Dust this language became more euphemistic, and the dust thus led to 'unnatural illness' not only because of its physical agents, but also because of its magical or spiritual components. The dread action of the dust caused such fear of being poisoned by slaves using it that 'poisoning' became a synonymous term for all manner of magical and spiritual acts done by African slaves. The myth of its power grew along with its reputation, and slowly it became something other than what it had started as, relegated to a world of purely magical practice with many of its original ingredients and the reasons for their use lost in the scurry of fame and time. However, before we dig deeper into such fertile earth, it is best to understand the origins of Goofer Dust and how those have influenced its development.

And His Name That Sat on Him was Death: Towards an Etymology

To better understand our mysterious 'hurting powder' one must first examine the origins of its rather strange name – "*Goofer.*" Although regional accents often render it as gopher or even goober, its proper name is goofer, the word goofer coming from the Bantu *kufua* and the Ki-Kongo *kufa,* both meaning, "*to die,*"[1] or "*from a bone,*" an interesting fact which as we can see was retained into the new world, "*They claim*

---

[1] Joseph E. Holloway and Vass, Winifred K., *The African Heritage of American English* (Indiana University Press: 1997), 98.

they'll make it from bones, dried bones from people. call it goofer dust at home. They sprinkle a little goofer dust in your tracks and you're sure going wrong."[2] Furthermore Robert Thompson, the American historian and writer specializing in the art of Africa and the Afro-Atlantic world, suggests that the verb *goof,* the adjective *goofy,* and perhaps even the slang expressions *goof off* and *goof on* may originate from some transferred sense like "be dead" or "dead-headed."[3] Linguistics is not my area of expertise, however it has been long known amongst older practitioners of hoodoo and Southern conjure that the root of saying that someone was "goofy" was because they had been 'goofered,' "*(Well, what is goofer supposed to be?) What they mean is to make you goofy. (Oh, it's goofy dust?) So now, say, for instance I want you to lose your memory, if you were going to court or something with [against] me - it would get you where you would probably forget what you's talking about."*[4] In 1938 the aforementioned informant, from Mobile Alabama, says Goofer Dust *"make [sic] you goofy."* The word "goofy" is used directly even though we are told that the first known use of the word comes from 1921[5]. The use of goofy is not unlike the term 'jake legged' meaning that someone was suffering from neurological paralysis caused by drinking improperly distilled or contaminated liquor – 'Jake.' Known in the United states simply as 'Jake,' the late 19th-century patent medicine Jamaica ginger extract provided a way to obtain alcohol during Prohibition, since it contained approximately 70% to 80%

---

[2] Informant from Snow Hill, Maryland. Harry Middleton Hyatt, *Hoodoo–Conjuration–Witchcraft–Rootwork*, vol.1, 225.

[3] Joey Lee Dillard and Linda L. Blanton, *Toward a Social History of American English* (De Gruyter Mouton: 2015), 200.

[4] Informant from Mobile, Alabama. Hyatt, vol.1, 226-227.

[5] Online Etymology Dictionary, s.v. "Goofy" accessed January 24, 2020. https://www.etymonline.com/word/goofy#etymonline_v_33708.

ethanol by weight.[6] The characteristic paralysis of the hands and feet brought about by bad 'Jake,' was an identifiable symptom of poisoned individuals, just as the befuddled, confused, and senseless behavior of a goofy person was an identifiable symptom of someone who had been 'goofered.'

The very word *"goofer"* and its adjective *"goofering"* is so inexorably linked to the practice of hoodoo and Southern conjure that it was a byword for the practice itself along with such terms as *"hoodoo," "tricking," "witching," "conjuring,"* or *"handicapping,'*[7] and the practitioner themselves known not only as *"root-doctor," "wood-doctor,"* and *"witchcraft-woman,"* but also as a *"goofer-doctor."*[8] It is worth noting that the term "goofer-doctor" was most popularly used in the Sea Islands along the Atlantic coast of the Southeastern United States.

We see however that this substance and its deadly nature did not originate within the United States but goes back to an earlier and much more lethal compound in Africa. This is something deeply important to the tradition of hoodoo and Southern conjure - a clear and direct African retention. In a tradition whose very strength is often that of its willingness to actively engage in admixture, Goofer Dust presents us with an essential origin back to Africa and immediately tells us much of its use - a poisonous compound used in Africa whose recipe was transferred to the Americas during the transatlantic slave trade taking with it its very name and adding that name into the normative langue of American culture.

---

[6] Leon Gussow, "The Jake Walk and Limber Trouble," *Emergency Medicine News* 26, no. 10 (2004), 48. https://doi.org/10.1097/00132981-200410000-00045.

[7] Newbell Niles Puckett, *Folk Beliefs of the Southern Negro* (1926), 197.

[8] E. C. Parsons, *Folk-Lore of (The Sea Islands, S. C, M. A.F.L. S.)*, vol. 16, (1923), 211-12.

Away! Thou'rt Poison to My Blood: Possible Medical Symptoms, Magic vs. Poison

How then is one goofered, and what does this bring about? Goofer Dust is primarily delivered by absorption through the feet of the intended target via direct skin contact. The dust is laid or scattered out where the person one wishes to goofer will walk through it, *"So he took this stuff [Goofer Dust] and sprinkled it all around the front porch and on the side of the front porch - sprinkled it around enough so he could walk in it when he come out."*[9] In older methods of deployment, Goofer Dust is not only placed along a person's path, but may also be laid down in a cross mark pattern or have cross marks drawn into it and is then spat upon to activate it. Other marks including a circle with an X inside it or three rows of wavy lines known as 'snake' marks/signs are also used, both of which herald back to the Nsibidi signs or ideograms of Africa.[10] This places goofering firmly within the realm of 'foot track magic,' of which one form is a means of delivering "magical poison" into a victim through their feet, causing an 'unnatural illness.'[11] The characteristic symptoms of such poisoning are sharp pains or itching in the feet or legs, followed by notable and painful swelling of the feet, legs, and lower extremities, an inability to walk, drowsiness, muddled thinking, and even death, *"You call it goofer dust. They take it - they puts it down and you're supposed to walk on it and if you walk on it, and it get on you, it will work through the sole of your shoe and it will commence to swelling. And it will make you drag, sick - sick, you know, sick with your leg - just cause it to swell and pain.*[12]*"*

---

[9] Hyatt, vol.1, 223.

[10] Debra Devi, *The Language of the Blues* (Billboard Books: 2006), 92.

[11] Devi, 96.

[12] Hyatt, *Hoodoo–Conjuration–Witchcraft–Rootwork*, vol.1, 785.

However, there is a belief that Goofer Dust is a purely "magical poison." This idea is most often promoted by the camp that identifies Goofer Dust and other situations such as 'Live Things in You' as being solely of a spiritual or magical nature or caused by misunderstood medical or psychological problems and often disregards any possible toxic or poisonous explanations. Subsequently, some noted sources in the tradition who follow this line of thinking suggest that the classic initial symptoms of being 'goofered' are merely "*those of diabetic edema and diabetic neuropathy*."[13]

This is a dismissive and ahistorical position, a position that denies not only the depth of the tradition, but also the very magical and spiritual power that the argument attempts to conceal itself behind. We see time and again people reporting illness and pain from exposure to Goofer Dust, being 'hurt' by it, and personal reports of loved ones, friends, or colleagues killed by it. Whereas it is true that Type 2 diabetes is currently an ongoing and prevalent problem not only within the United States, but particularly within the African American community, it must be remembered that many of these reports come from a much earlier age when Type 2 diabetes was not as widespread as it is today. To suggest that even earlier those people living under chattel slavery were simply suffering from diabetes is not only insulting but preposterous. Tossing aside the possibility that early compounds of Goofer Dust were recreations with available materials of an earlier African poison and suggesting that these cases are just common people reporting harm due to a lack of understanding of ordinary medical complaints is truly 'throwing the baby out with the bathwater.'

Such controversies aside, we see that the deployment of and resulting symptoms from Goofer Dust suggest a solid

---

[13] Catherine Yronwode, *Goofer Dust* (1994-2019). Retrieved from http://www.luckymojo.com/gooferdust.html.

possibility that the substance is, just as it was always described, a strong, possibly neurological poison. The initial pains and itches brought on by the substance's immediate entry into the body via the feet or legs, the swelling of the feet and legs, the onset of drowsiness, muddled thinking, mental confusion, sexual impotence, symptoms similar to gout, high blood pressure, and angina all speak to a potential poisoning affecting the cardiovascular and related systems. Further reports of a general ill luck, a menacing aspect being against one's life, or being troubled by negative spirits are also reported following the initial physical symptoms. Certainly, as time went on there were greater reports of a magical 'poisoning' and less reports of symptoms relating to a physical poisoning, but this is easily understood as a movement away from the older recipes, for various reasons including loss of source, inability to acquire needed materia, and legal ramifications, and as we will see later more stringent methods for the interment of the dead. As these factors increased, we see the change of attitudes about Goofer Dust from a notoriously poisonous substance to a baleful magical substance and finally to a magical compound that ritual alone activates.

True Apothecary thy Drugs art Quick: Substance and Recipes for Goofer Dust

The original African recipe for *kufa dust* is, to the best of my knowledge, no longer known, or at least it is unavailable to those uninitiated in traditional African Sorcerous Societies, however we do have a good number of recipes both modern and antique from the Southern United States. These recipes most often call for graveyard dirt or clay, powdered snake or lizard heads and snake sheds, powdered scorpions and other insects (normally venomous ones), as well as powdered insect nests or larvae, powdered steel or anvil dust or grease, black and red pepper, salt, charcoal, and brick dust. The variety of materia used in these recipes can be rather peculiar in nature without some kind of framework upon which to hang them. Originally the framework is a poisonous compound which effects one by direct skin contact, resulting in damage to the neurological and cardiological systems; that was then replaced by a framework attempting to recreate this substance at a later date within the new world, and then finally one of a purely magical nature without direct attempt to create a medically poisonous compound. Viewing the suggested materia through the lens of these three frameworks is beneficial to our understanding of how Goofer Dust may function both as a physical compound and as a cultural artifact.

Primary Materia:

Graveyard Dirt: Often seen as the chief ingredient in Goofer Dust - so much so that in many cases they are used interchangeably: *"It will be noted how frequently graveyard dust is required in the practice of hoodoo, goofer dust as it is often called,"*[14] *"That's what we call that graveyard clay, goofer dust."*[15] There are a variety of reasons for the use of graveyard dirt in Goofer Dust, but as a primary ingredient within the compounding framework of a poisonous recipe, its use is due to the fact that it was often poisonous. Graveyards of the past experienced ground contamination because of decomposing bodies being buried in simple coffins or placed directly into the earth. It is partially this contamination, either by decay or disease, that led to substances like graveyard dirt and dust being

---

[14] Zora Neale Hurston, "Hoodoo in America," *The Journal of American Folklore*, vol. 44, no. 174, (Oct.-Dec., 1931), 397.

[15] Informant from Florence, South Carolina, Hyatt, *Hoodoo–Conjuration–Witchcraft–Rootwork*, vol.1, 224.

categorized as 'poisonous,' because they often carried disease germs from the bodies that had decayed in them[16]: *"They take graveyard dirt, they say, and make goofer dust out of it and gave you a lingering cough."*[17] It is this inherent poisonous or contaminative nature that makes it first amongst equals as a part of the needed materia to compound Goofer Dust, *"Graveyard dirt and different things mixed together is goofer dust."*[18] We so often see graveyard dirt, dust, or clay alone being called Goofer Dust that it cannot help but harken back to the African origin of the word, *kufua* or *kufa, "to die,"* and thus being of or belonging to the dead.

Snakes: One of the essential ingredients is snakes in one form or another, either the powdered head or body or the shed skin of a snake after molting. In earlier recipes there is a greater call for the powdered heads of venomous snakes, *"Goofer dust is snake head,"*[19] *"It's a rattlesnake dust,"*[20] *"they take serpents heads and grind them up and powder them up and they supposed to bury that under your doorstep. That's goofer dust,"*[21] *"you get a snake - you can take a rattlesnake and dry his head up, pound it up, and then you can go to work and use that as goofer dust. Kill anybody."*[22] The snakes desired are venomous, often rattlesnake, but others also appear, *"Goofer dust is made up out of... gets a blacksnake*[23] *before it mates - catch him long about in March, just*

---

[16] Charles Porterfield, "The Conjurer's Garden," Paper to the 2020 International Necromancy Consortium, (unpublished).

[17] Informant from Elizabeth City, North Carolina, 224.

[18] Informant from Mobile, Alabama

[19] Informant from Fayetteville, North Carolina, 225.

[20] Informant from New Orleans, Louisiana, 225.

[21] Informant from Warrenton Virginia.

[22] Informant from Waycross, Georgia.

[23] This is one of the common names for Agkistrodon piscivorus, a species of pit

long about March. Hang him upsides down [tail up, head down] and cut his throat and let his blood drip and have his blood drip into a jar. ... Take this snake and let him dry up and after he dry up, you grind that blacksnake - the whole skin and all, and make a powder."[24]

Here just as with graveyard dirt we on occasion see ground or powdered snake's head being referred to per ipsum as Goofer Dust. What is interesting in this is that these are the powdered heads or bodies of venomous snakes that have been dried out without any discussion of removal of fangs or venom producing parts of their anatomy before they are ground to dust, thus producing a material powder that may still contain poisonous material even if greatly reduced in nature. Also, we find that the most of these snakes are of the Viperidae family; various species of rattlesnakes and cottonmouths. The Viperid venoms typically contain protein-degrading enzymes, called proteases, that produce symptoms such as pain, strong local swelling and necrosis, and blood loss from cardiovascular damage, symptoms not unlike those reported, although to a lesser extent, from Goofer Dust. Certainly, there are no rattlesnakes in Africa and the place of the rattlesnake in hoodoo and Southern conjure is quite correctly cited as evidence of hoodoo's American origins and admixture make up. However, the rattlesnake is a viper, and there are numerous vipers indigenous to Africa and Western Africa whose head shapes and color patterns are not unlike many of the varieties of North American rattlesnakes. As we start to encounter recipes further from the Eastern sea coast of the United States and from later dates, we no longer see dried venomous snakes or their heads being called for, but instead simply snake sheds of no particular species. This is indicative of the slow change to the basic form of Goofer Dust from

---

viper in the subfamily Crotalinae of the family Viperidae most commonly known in the United States as the cottonmouth.

[24] Female informant, age 68, from Richmond, Virginia, Georgia. Hyatt, 293.

medically poisonous substance to purely ritual element.

Scorpions and other insects: Several different kinds of insects are called for as an ingredient in Goofer Dust in various recipes, but most of them are venomous, *"Goofer dust is snake head, scorpion head, lizard head - listen, snake head dust, scorpion dust and lizard dust. That's what you call goofer dust You get them things and you kill them and you cut the heads off and you dry that. After you dry that, you powder that up. That's what they call goofer dust,"*[25] *"Goofer dust is graveyard dust and any dust from a poison insect mixed together,"*[26] *"Goofer dust is dust from any live insect."*[27] Again, as we distance ourselves from the Atlantic coast of the United States, we start to detect a change in the recipe, *"That's just this fine dirt. (Goofer dust is almost anything put down.) Anything that would be to have influence - like you get from this dirt dauber nest and the pepper I told you about and mix it up, that would be goofer dust."*[28] In this example we are advised to use a dirt dauber, a name commonly applied to a number of wasps from either the family Sphecidae or Crabronidae that build their nests from mud. Dirt or mud daubers are not normally aggressive, but they can become belligerent when threatened. It is uncommon to be stung by one, and any pain caused by their sting is not considered especially painful. However, it is interesting to note that as insects which might be observed in nature for possible use in Goofer Dust, the female mud dauber sting paralyzes her prey (primarily spiders), preserving them until her offspring are ready to eat them. It may be argued that those observing this took the venom of this insect to be a paralytic.

---

[25] Informant from Fayetteville, North Carolina, 225.

[26] Informant is a profession root doctor from Sumter, South Carolina. Hyatt, vol.2, 1439.

[27] Informant is from Charleston, South Carolina, vol.1, 226.

[28] Informant from Mobile, Alabama.

Secondary Materia:

Anvil dust: Anvil or steel dust is often seen as an ingredient in a variety of compounds, and this is true of Goofer Dust as well, *"Goofer dust is nothing but anvil dust. Anvil dust will work any trick, and that's goofer dust. They have a new way of calling it, the Rosicrucians*[29] *do. We don't call it goofer dust, we call it anvil dust. That's the same as the goofer dust, it's the same thing. It'll work tricks in every way. Just whatever you want do that goofer dust does it, but it's called anvil dust now. We don't use the name of goofer dust. They don't allow us to say hoodoo, or we are not allowed to say goofer dust."*[30] Madame Collins' comments are particularly interesting: *"We don't use the name of goofer dust. They don't allow us to say hoodoo, or we are not allowed to say goofer dust."* It is difficult here to determine if she means the general culture around her in Memphis, Tennessee, or the Rosicrucian Order to which she was associated. Anvil dust is often used to empower compounds being made, and it was greatly sought after, *"Anvil dust is also greatly valued as conjure material. One educated blacksmith of Columbus, Miss., tells me that people are constantly coming into his shop to get the black flakes that fall from the hot iron when it is pounded, although they always look ashamed and give a fictitious reason as to why they want it."*[31] We often see the mention of anvil dust explained as an ingredient from those who have taken to calling any dust compound used in hoodoo 'goofer dust,' *"Well, you can get steel dust - mostly any dust, you understand, that you mix. (They call that*

---

[29] Madam Collins told Hyatt that she had studied spiritual work by mail order and had received a diploma from the Rosicrucian Order, AMORC in San Jose, California ("de White Brothers").

[30] Informant is Mrs. /Madam Collins. Spiritual Doctor. 651 Stephens St., Memphis, Tennessee. Hyatt, vol.2, 1019.

[31] Puckett, 237.

goofer dust?) Yes sir, that's the meaning of goofer dust."[32] It may be that the addition of anvil dust was an abrasive which aided in delivering the other toxic substances through the skin.

Tertiary Materia:

Black and red pepper and salt: We now enter into materia sometimes called for in recipes of Goofer Dust that are from the group of recipes that generally consider any magically compounded powder in hoodoo or Southern conjure to be *"goofer dust," "That's something the same thing that ah have just told you - what you make up, pepper and salt. (That's all goofer dust - any kind of dust?) Yeah, any kind of dust,"*[33] *"Well, goofer - this stuff a graveyard dirt, red pepper and black pepper. I call all that stuff - you can get a snail and powder him - all of them goofer dust." (Why do they call it goofer?) Call it goofer - it do things that you can't just [do with] ordinary things can do."*[34] The last example appears to be a very watered down version of Goofer Dust, yet it still contains graveyard dirt for its possible contaminative nature, but then adds in red and black pepper as possible irritants and powdered snail dust as an 'insectile' component. Snails are seen in hoodoo as drying up a person's sexual nature, so it is at least being used here as an organism that is known to stop or dry up personal health or nature.

Brick dust and charcoal: Here we have more examples of recipes that consider any powdered item to be a Goofer Dust, *"Take that charcoal - brick dust and charcoal. You know, anything you beat up and make a dust out of it, that goofer dust."*[35] The only

---

[32] Informant from New Orleans, Louisiana, 226.

[33] Informant from Savannah, Georgia, 225.

[34] Informant from Little Rock, Arkansas.

[35] Informant from Vicksburg, Mississippi, 226.

possible connection that this might have to harmful or contaminative ingredients is a well-known fact amongst older masons and bricklayers that care must be shown when working with older 'soft' style red bricks. The reason for this is if they were used as a part of buildings such as hospitals or mortuaries the bricks can release biological toxins when broken or crumbled up. In fact, a bricklayer known to the author contracted scarlet fever from working with older red bricks taken from a historic New Orleans hospital during remodeling. It is not impossible to suggest that well-known fact amongst laborers may be the cause of the addition of ground up red bricks in some recipes for Goofer Dust, but it seems unlikely as the recipes do not specifically call for bricks from such places where they might have 'soaked up' toxins or disease germs.

Rare but Telling Materia:

Devil's snuff: Very rarely we see mention of "devil's snuff" called for in certain hoodoo compounds or works, *"You go in the woods and we got what they call the devil's snuff - you seen that haven't you... You take that and powder it up and you use that with your lodestone...(They call that goofer dust down in Louisiana.) Yes."* [36] Searching for this particular ingredient is a rather difficult path to follow, but we are given some clues along the way by Hyatt, *"[Devil's snuff originally was the powder from puffballs - various fungi of the family Lycoperdaceae (class Basidiomycetes) - globular shaped, discharging ripe spores when pressed. As a boy I found their brown powder or smoke interesting, though warned that it was poisonous, and did not know puffballs were mushrooms. The plant must have been specially created for old-fashioned rootmen, but I suspect enterprising hoodoo drug stores in*

[36] Informant from Memphis, Tennessee. Hyatt, vol.5, 4245.

later years manufactured a devil's snuff of their own.]"[37] Most puffballs are not poisonous, however some are visually similar to young agarics, especially the lethal Amanitas, such as the death cap or destroying angel mushrooms. One cannot help but wonder if the addition of devil's snuff, a common name in the Southern United States for several different puffballs, was an attempt to add a poisonous component.

Devil's grass: "I have heard that goofer dust is just different roots for whatever kind of work it is you wanted to do or anything bad; that's the kind of roots that you would get. There's some kind of a root - devil grass root. (It has no other name?) No other name. Take devil grass and snake's head and grind it up together and make a powder out of it. See, for instance, if you wanted to hurt someone or something other like that, and sprinkle it in their hat, the band of their hat. It would run them blind."[38] This recipe calls for the snake's heads from our primary ingredients, but adds "Devil's grass." Devil's grass is a common name in the Southern United States for several different plants, but most notably are Jimson Weed (Datura stramonium) and Bermuda grass (Cynodon dactylon). We do not know which of these the informant is suggesting for use, but both can produce toxic effects. However, it is likely that this is Cynodon dactylon being spoken of, as it is used in numerous other hoodoo recipes under its other names couch grass and witch grass. The chief point is that we see again materia that could produce toxic or poisonous results against an intended victim.

---

[37] Informant is Hyatt himself, 3806-3807.

[38] Informant from Wilson, North Carolina. Hyatt, vol.1, 225.

The Dose Makes the Poison: Uses of Goofer Dust in Hoodoo and Southern Conjure

The most common use of Goofer Dust is by deploying it so that an intended victim walks through or over the dust and comes into contact with it via the feet or lower legs, *"You're supposed to walk over that,"*[39] *"The home that you want to put the bad luck on, see. And then you begin the seven steps back you begin sprinkling your what they call goofer dust. See, that's the beginning of the hard luck."*[40] Also it may be deployed directly into the footwear of one's intended victim, *"I have heard that conjure doctors put goofer dust in your shoes to put affliction on you and sometimes it causes you to have a bad foot, a sore foot. It'll never be healed, a swelling or something, unless you go to another conjure doctor."*[41] It should be noted that this 'dosing' or 'tricking' of shoes is a work from a later period of time after shoe ownership and wearing was common. In earlier times many people did not own shoes or only had one pair reserved for special situations, and during these times exposing others to Goofer Dust via their bare feet was a simple matter.

Because contact through the feet is so common, the various attempted cures for being 'goofered' address these parts of the body before all others, *"He was told...trim his corns and trim his toenails. He told him to keep his toenails short because the goofer dust would get under his toenails and it was harder and cost him more to get it out - to git the spell off him if it got under his toenails."*[42] However, we do also see that contact need not be through the feet alone if one can get it to a target another way,

---

[39] Informant from Warrenton, Virginia.

[40] Informant from Jacksonville, Florida, 224.

[41] Informant from Ocean City, Maryland, 227.

[42] Informant from Richmond, Virginia, 289.

"... put it in the mattress of a person where that they have to sleep on, and you [the victim] supposed to just go away – just pine away."[43]

Later substances called Goofer Dust are said to be burned or carried, kept in 'hands' or 'mojo bags,' but these uses characterize materia that had become synonymously described as Goofer Dust and generally do not resemble the substance. Goofer Dust as an original poisonous product is always deployed, in one way or another, towards its intended target so that they will have direct bodily contact with the powder.

O Death, Where Is Thy Sting? O Grave, Where Is Thy Victory: Conclusion

The author has attempted in his own meager way to make the case that Goofer Dust was in the beginning a poisonous substance with magical or spiritual overtones, originating in Western Africa and coming to the United States via the transatlantic slave trade. Its name, substance, and use help to prove this, if only in some small way, and only later did it slowly transform into a non-poisonous, purely ritual or magical substance.

It is clear that Goofer Dust was a central part of hoodoo and Southern conjure, particularly in the Sea Islands and the Eastern Atlantic coast of the United States, so much so that its name became synonymous with the very practice and tradition. This synonymous nature and naming, along with difficulties preserving specific recipes within a primarily oral tradition, troubles obtaining needed components, and possible legal repercussions, allowed the name Goofer Dust to come to mean any and all powders used within the tradition. *Goofering*

[43] Informant from Memphis, Tennessee, 227.

and *goofered* lost their specific 'hurt' meanings and became any influence or person under the influence of a spell; the *goofer-man* and *goofer-doctor* simply became another name for the root-man and conjure doctor. As this change gained momentum the inevitable occurred - the once lethal *kufua dust* became a purely magical and ritual substance no more toxic than a handful of field dirt.

As this inevitable 'watering down' of the famous dust grew, many people, even those within the tradition, began to relegate it to being something that either killed by force of magic or simply did not kill at all. This pulled back a curtain onto some of the practices within the tradition of hoodoo and Southern conjure. When we begin to attempt to internally discount the very practices and substances of the tradition via cynical materialism, one is left wondering why practice it at all? In fact, a few years ago the author encountered a package of "Goofer Dust" that was a fine powder the texture of incense grade sawdust, colored a vivid primary blue, that smelled strongly of root beer! How the mighty have fallen indeed!

The author's background is not in neurotoxins, ethnobotany, or entheogens. He is by trade and inclination simply a conjure doctor, a fortunate participant in a vibrant, living tradition. A tradition that can often be frustrating and confusing to navigate through. A tradition that also has its fair share of loud, absolute experts who do not dare to be questioned, but when it comes to matters such as these, matters that are rooted in African retentions and origins within the tradition, matters that speak to the power and knowledge of the early practitioners of the tradition, we owe it to the tradition and those who executed it to at least contemplate what may have been. To those that scoff at the idea of an African poison being retained and used in the Americas I say to you in the words of Cromwell, *"I beseech you, in the bowels of Christ, think it possible that you may be mistaken."*

The Making of Magical Inks

Richard Spelker

The making and use of magical inks dates back to the obscure pre-history of humanity. The origin of writing ink will probably remain unknown, but historically scholars place its first usage in writing back to 2500 BCE in ancient Egypt or perhaps even earlier to ancient China.[1]

There is very little written about the subject of making magical inks, its invisibility in history was because it was so common to the practitioners who used ink, and they likely kept their magical formulas secret. Likely standard ink was used being purchased from stationers and traders throughout history. It's not hard to imagine the instinctive impulse to draw, make a mark or even doodle as a mnemonic to mark an important memory or useful bit of information. Clearly with writing there is a willful intent behind it. Ink is one trail where the magical practitioner's will, is evident. The use of plants in making magical inks can be used in written charms and spells. However, this paper will not cover written charms and spells, as that is a larger subject that will be covered in future presentations.

While colored mineral pigments often need nothing to retain their brilliant colors, plants used in ink making need mordants to preserve their color. Mordants are salts with metals in them used to preserve the color of plant materials,

---

[1] Carvalho

much in the same way as mummies were preserved in ancient Egypt. There is an uncanniness of opening a medieval manuscript and seeing plant colors which illustrate the interiors, looking much in the same way they did a thousand years ago, not quite dead in their tomb like enclosures. It is always wondrous how such vibrancy still persists. The magic in using plant-based inks preserved with mordants, is that a magical practitioner's intention will long live on in their working, giving subtle energy to their work.

Making a Good Ink

I have been researching and making writing inks for over 25 years and have collected well over a thousand recipes, many that claimed to be excellent inks ended up with contrary results. Having studied art materials for most of my life, I have come to expect a certain high quality in what I make and use. The recipes on the internet are generally atrocious and appear to celebrate their shortcomings.

Before we can talk about what makes a good and effective magical writing ink, it is important to understand what makes a good basic writing ink. Before 1800, all good writing ink formulas were discovered by accident. Every community developed an ink from mostly local ingredients and every so often used exotic ingredients from other parts of the world, such as dragon's blood resin from the Near East and indigo from the Far East. Ink recipes whether in personal handwritten recipe books or published formularies, were known to be uncertain and likely unreliable. After reviewing the ink formulas I have collected, mostly published in authoritative books, I have often wondered if anyone actually tried to make the recipes. Some authors of these formularies have assured us of the most excellent recipes that on closer inspection clearly can't work; the recipes seem to be incomplete, deceptive or more likely, regurgitated from earlier formularies. About 1890, scientific researchers started an effort to determine just what made for a quality ink.

A good writing ink should be a liquid coloring madder that is brilliant, permanent, and fulfills its intended purpose with perfect fluidity. More specifically, a good black writing ink should flow readily from the pen, penetrate the paper surface, indicate a black color in a short period of time, be durable, not corrode metal pen tips, not destroy the paper written on, be without sediment, and has permanence based on chemical and not just pigmentary qualities.[2]

Historical magical ink recipes

The internet and popular occult books that offer magical ink making recipes are mostly poor examples of what a good ink should be. It makes me wonder if these authors had any success with their efforts or if they even made them at all. It appears that most of the recipes on the internet as of 2020 are derived from Herman Slater's formula book, discussed further on.

The basic ingredients for a magical ink should be its writability, color, scent, and magical inclusions. All these ingredients work together by the guiding philosophy that these ingredients would work in sympathy with the forces of the Natural, Divine or Infernal forces to achieve the magical outcome desired. As in the Pact with the Devil Ink, I would think the Devil would want the ink to be archival, so as not to fade away by Judgement Day. Of course, the supreme ink would be one's own blood, intentions can't be more serious than that! The colors, scents and magical inclusions depend on the magical tradition in question for use, these elements or correspondences vary from tradition to tradition and from

[2] Hopkins, 268.

author to author: modern and ancient. The best solution to finding the right recipe is to formulate a magical ink for yourself that corresponds best with your tradition and practice.

Blood as Ink

Whenever the topic of magical inks is considered, there is the inevitable question about the use of blood as ink. Blood can certainly be believed to be the first original ink. It is connected to the Faust legends and magical pacts in general: blood is the philosophical gnomon upon which the whole business of magical ink use rotates.

The use of blood in magic today is still a transgressive subject that evokes strong emotions within the magical community. Despite its moral controversy, there is something rather atavistic about the use of blood even if it's contingent on an accidental cut or nosebleed, that feeling that the vital fluid should not be wasted. For me there is a certain horror and fascination of seeing a wadded-up paper towel with my blood on it: a sense of displacement and loss unless it's put to good use. Reactions to the use of blood in art ranges from horror and disgust to a sublime atavism that deepens the artist's spirituality.

John Kieschnick in his "Blood Writing in Chinese Buddhism" [3] states one of the most common forms of ascetic practice in Chinese Buddhism involves pricking one's tongue or finger to draw blood which is then mixed with ink and used to copy Buddhist scriptures. His descriptions of the use of blood in pious religious writing can be said as being harrowing and gruesome. A sixteenth century monk named Hanshaw Deging describes in his autobiography his reasons

---

[3] Kieschnick.

for writing in his own blood:

> *"In the Spring of my thirty-second year, I returned from Yanmen. At this time, I recalled the benevolence of my [deceased] parents and the care they had given me. I also thought of all of the obstacles that stood between me and the [Buddha] Law. On reading the vow of the great master Huisi of Nanyue, I vowed to make a copy of the Scripture of the Expanse of Buddhas of the Flower Adornment (i.e. the Avatamsaka) by mixing my own blood with gold. Above, this would tie me to the karma of prajna, and below it would repay my parents for their benevolence."*[4]

It was thought that mixing one's blood with gold and writing out scripture would connect with one's parents and offer merit to them in order to achieve a better afterlife. This could be done by anyone, not just a nun or monk. Often, devout Buddhist monks would take likely symbolic scripture literally and go all the way as a practice for virtuous self-sacrifice, from the Avatamsaka Sutra, 7th century: "Cut away your skin for paper, draw your blood for ink and use your marrow for water. Break off a piece of your own bone for a pen and copy out the Buddhist precepts...This was the most extreme of practice where fingers were cut off in self-sacrifice..."[5]

From my reading, the most extreme magical practitioner of blood magic today is the Sorceress Cagliastro whose magical practice centers around the use of her blood. She offers two blood ink recipes: "You will need to write your Creed... Place no fewer than seven drops of the Sacred Elixir from your writing hand into your ink... it takes a significant

[4] ibid.

[5] ibid.

accumulation to do so [in writing out one's Creed.] Accumulate and refrigerate or freeze it until you have enough.[6]"

"Any of these Elixirs can be added to ink [blood harvested from different parts of the body. To do so, add them to a black ink, preferably one with mercury, and using a hide or parchment from an animal and a freshly cut quill...[7]"

A recipe for blood ink? Many online magical writers are somewhat firmly against the use of blood in magical practice, only a non-blood-based substitute is acceptable, such as plant or artificial coloring and symbolic additives. There are very few magical practitioners who are serious about using blood, let alone sharing recipes for it. One amusing bit of advice was from the Usenet page alt.lucky.w in 1999. I print the posting in full for effect[8]:

> *"Sour salt, citric Acid is the anticoagulant of choice in inks made of blood, human or otherwise. Make a saturated solution of citric acid, which you can find labeled as sour salt in the Kosher food section of your supermarket. Add three drops to each approximate teaspoon of blood. (30ml) You may need more, but this much, if mixed in, will allow you to add more if needed.*
>
> *Dove's blood ink is best made from ripe pokeberries, which is what it was originally made from. This is a very permanent ink, samples of which over two hundred years old are still quite legible.*
>
> *Do not use enamel coated paper. Ok for parchment and papyrus however.*
>
> *Bat's blood ink should be drawn from the heart of the living bat by use of a hypodermic needle. If you are using this to make a Lamen for summoning, be careful that the drawing of the ink is done in*

[6] Sorceress Cagliastro, 34.

[7] ibid, 55.

[8] Email correspondence,"To: alt.lucky.w, From: "[John, last name deleted]" Subject: Re: recipe for blood ink? Accessed: Tue, 21 Sep 1999.

the appropriate day and hour. You can keep it from coagulating by putting a ml of the citric acid solution into the hypodermic beforehand.

Wolfs blood ink should be drawn from the aorta of the wolf, it's in about the same place it is on humans.

Regards, John"

Unfortunately, John's original recipe for dove's blood ink in ancient Egypt was actual dove's blood. This is the only claim of connection I have seen between poke berries and dove's blood. Another criticism is "what bat" and "what wolf" is John drawing blood from? It would seem that to be an effective magical practitioner, one would also need to have exceptional animal stalking and wrangling talents. Such seeming hyperbole discredits a plausible method for preserving blood for magical ink use.

Blood ink could be beyond the happy intention of a magical ink maker and it's suggested by Louis Martinie, a magical practitioner in New Orleans as he relates "...a red liquid [such as a commercial red ink pen] carries the power of human blood and is or becomes, in a very real sense, blood.[9]" With that in mind, there are alternatives to actual blood in making, as plant based "blood" inks.

Indigo Inks

After reading many comments online concerning magical spells, there appears to be a need among magical practitioners to find a plant-based alternative to blood in making "blood" inks. This substitution was considered by the ancients as in the Greek Magical Papyri. This is an amazing list of

---

[9] Rodgers 88

euphemistic replacement names of herbs and stones for animal parts: these definitions were considered secret. While not an exhaustive list, it does include such plant substitutions for blood as: lupine, wild lettuce, cedar, mulberry sap, wild garlic, chamomile, bear's breech, tamarisk gall, and wormwood.[10] One herb that is often overlooked as an alternative to blood is indigo. This has been one of the paramount textile dyes from ancient times and has been associated with magic and death. Woad is an ancient blue dye plant that is similar to indigo in chemistry except woad lacks indigo's intensity. The Vikings, who used both woad and indigo, associated the color blue, according to Icelandic sagas, with the goddess of death[11]. In Indonesia, the native people there have developed a complex belief around the use of indigo. This magical plant is considered as the blue medicine: "Women in Kodi are associated with the "blue arts" of witchcraft, indigo dyeing, and herbalism. Hereditary witches have "blueness in them," they are "bluish people"...whose very blood is believed to be in some way poisonous to others.[12]" Research suggests that:

> *"Menstrual blood is called "blood from the womb"...and is said to dry into the bluish black color of a deep indigo dye...Female herbalists and midwives... compare the menstrual flow to the dyes fermenting in the indigo, certain roots and barks are used both to control the bleeding of colors to control the bleeding of women's bodies.[13]"*

---

[10] Betz, PGM XII. 401-44.

[11] Balfour-Paul, 25.

[12] Hoskins.

[13] ibid.

Perhaps the reason to not consider using indigo as a magical ink is the seemingly very complex methods for making dried indigo to become water-soluble. Unlike textile processing which would require a cauldron of indigo dye and a naturally weeks long process, there is a quick modern way to make indigo water soluble in small batches.

Water Soluble Indigo

To 100 parts water add 20 parts sodium hydroxide. Then, add 10 parts indigo powder and 20 parts iron sulphate. Combine the second to the first together. Bottle, shake, and wait for two days.[14] This formula results in a thick paste, when water and gum arabic are added makes for a wonderful dark blue ink. Another example is an indigo ink for spiritual piety from Tibet contains the soot of one's own hair:[15]

Singed Hair Indigo Ink.

The recipe gives no measurements. The ink maker is to burn some of their own hair and mix the resulting soot with soluble indigo and goat's milk as an adhesive binder.

The Murky World of Dragon's Blood Ink.

Of all the magical ink recipes, the popular and significant ones are the three modern "blood" inks: Dove's Blood Ink, Bat's Blood Ink, and Dragon's Blood Ink. These have only been known to exist since the 1970's contrary to the contention that they have been around for hundreds or thousands of years. I

---

[14] Recipe given to author by James Stroud, chemist, 1993.

[15] Helman-Ważny, 99-101.

have done a deep dive into these much in demand inks and have found their history to be uncertain. After surveying all the blood ink recipes online and various popular occult books, it seems that all the recipes go back to Herman Slater and his Magickal Childe bookstore in New York City. I have discovered 54 blood ink recipes that use dragon's blood resin as their primary ingredient. After studying all the recipes, it appears that the original source of these ink recipes come from Slater's Magickal Formulary Spellbook, Book 1[16] first published in 1981. At this time, I have found only one modern reference to "blood" ink formulas prior to this, however it's possible that these ink recipes may have circulated in various magical communities and published in witchcraft publications that I haven't seen. No one seems to know the origins of Slater's ink formulas. The only reference I have found to date from modern times regarding dragon's blood before 1981 is a pamphlet: *Legends of Incense, Herb, and Oil Magic* by Lewis de Claremont from 1936.[17] De Claremont's book is a strange farrago of hoodoo root-working lore, sprinkled with a few recipes and references. It does mention dragon, bat and dove blood oils, but not inks.

Looking back at ancient history Pliny, Philo, Dioscorides. and Pseudo Dioscorides talk about dragon's blood resin with brief descriptions of its medical and artistic use. The next period in history where dragon's blood resin pops up is Renaissance Italy in formulary books having to do on making varnishes, such as the Bolognese Manuscript. ca. 1450 and the Paduan Manuscript from 1584. From the time of the Italian Renaissance until the 1970s in New York City the only use for dragon's blood I have found is in varnishes used by furniture and musical instrument makers, and perhaps after reading Pliny, Slater's imagination turned to purchasing

---

16 Slater.

17 De Claremont.

resins from local violin makers…possibly. The following are recipes given by Herman Slater for his "blood inks" with my comments to follow each recipe:

Dragon's Blood Ink

Dragon's blood resin	*1 part*
Alcohol	*15 parts*
Gum Arabic	*1 part*

Dragon's blood resin first comes to our attention historically in ancient Greek times. Pliny in his *Natural History* illustrates the origin of dragon's blood resin, that on an island near India there was an epic fight between an elephant and a giant snake, both died in the struggle and the mixture of the two bodies crushed together created dragon's blood resin. Since Pliny's time this myth has transformed into a history of incredible confusion. This giant snake in greek is called drakon, during the middle ages in the western Europe, the word became conflated with mythical dragons and the original notion of a giant snake was lost. Since ancient times, dragon's blood resin was traded to the West, without the buyers knowing the exact origin or even what plant it was from. It is still a disputed contention as to what plant Pliny was talking about, or if it was even a plant. Dragon's blood could have been the name of several different plants and materials. The Greek word 'drakontion' was also identified with cinnabar or mercury sulphide. In Spain in the Roman times, red lead oxide was also identified with the word cinnabar. The confusion becomes worse with Pliny writing in his *Natural History* about artist materials and medical remedies where the meaning of the words for certain materials are identified, cinnabar could mean dragon's blood resin, mercury sulfide, lead oxide, or even the plants snakeroot or dragon lily. Today we now know dragon's blood resin to be Sanguis Draconis or Cinnabaris from the island of Socotra in the Indian Ocean. A writer in the first century called Socotra "Snake Island." Naturalists in the 19th century confused this with other dragon's blood resins in Asia such as Pterocarpus Draco and Dracena Draco, but the true resin that gives the bright red dye is the Cinnabaris.[18]

Slater, in his *Magical Formulary Spellbook* gives vague and confusing uses for Dragon's blood ink, such as, uncrossing hexes, peace of mind, love, and even to be worked at midnight in a cemetery. His recipe is very basic and offers no advice on how to make it. Since the introduction of this recipe to the magical community, the uses for this ink have expanded to adding firepower of potency to amulets and spells for protection, energy, and purification, astral travel, love, marriage proposals, and reproductive issues, the formula is also said to stop diarrhea, bleeding, and as a cure for syphilis.

Considering the recipes read online, it seems that few of the authors ever tried to make the various "blood' inks. Many of the recipes are lifted from earlier sources leading back to Slater. Many of these recipes have the fatal flaw of trying to mix dragon's blood resin with water. Dragon's blood resin is only alcohol and essential oil soluble. What usually occurs is an expensive sticky mess that is difficult to handle, write with, and doesn't conform to what makes a good ink. These recipes are acceptable if one is working in a very messy and effluvial manner. The online results look more like a crime scene, than a magical working. Another problem is that even though alcohol will dissolve the resin, the color takes on a murky brownish red rather than the brilliant crimson of the

[18] Trinquier.

resin itself. After adding the water-soluble gum arabic, the solution becomes a clotted mess. Denise Alvarado states in *Hoodoo Voodoo Spellbook*[19] that it breaks from the ink contention that Slater created and uses standard red ink with dragon's blood resin as an inclusion, just floating around with a few drops of essential oil, and from my point of view, that could be sufficient enough. Everyone I know that has tried to recreate one of Slater's ink recipes and those descended from them, meets with dissatisfaction.

Bat's Blood Ink

Dragon's blood resin	*2 parts*
Myrrh resin	*0.5 part*
Cinnamon oil	*2 drops*
Indigo color	*2 drops*
Alcohol	*12 parts*
Gum Arabic	*0.5 part*

Even though Bat's blood ink is very similar to Dragon's blood ink as they both contain dragon's blood resin, the use of this ink is said not only to be sinister but dangerous. Slater warns us that this is for hexing people using baneful spirits. Since Slater's original formulation, this ink has expanded its purpose by other authors for spells of mystery, spells of darkness, for all things hidden, necromancy, domination, commanding, cursing, for misfortune and creating havoc…or merely communicating with one's ancestors. Going back to

[19] Alvarado.

ancient Egypt, bat's blood itself was used for swollen eyes and for creating amulets of deception. For the ancients it certainly had a most malevolent use, the ancient hermetic book *The Magick of Kiranis* and *Harpocraton,* also known to scholars as the *Cyranides,* a rarely discussed Greek magical text from the fourth century, contains a very early use for Bat's blood that I cannot help but read as a rape spell: "...if one will take the Blood of it [bat's blood] in a Cloth, and lay under a Woman's head, she not knowing it, if a Man lie with her, she will presently conceive. And it has other Efficacies, which I will now conceal; for I must not publish them."[20]

Dove's Blood Ink

Dragon's blood resin	*1 part*
Cinnamon oil	*2 drops*
Bay oil	*2 drops*
Alcohol	*10 parts*
Gum Arabic	*1 part*
Rose oil	*2 drops*

This dove's blood ink is again similar to the other Slater inks that use dragon's blood resin. Slater states its use for protection, peace of mind, and love. As the subject of love is a very important topic in magical workings, practitioners since Slater have been content with his suggestions for use. When looking at all the variations of these "blood" inks, the basis for these inks are dragon's blood resin and cinnamon oil. The

---

[20] Kirani, Book II, N.

only difference is that bat's blood inks have added indigo, and dove's blood inks have the addition of bay and rose oils.

Possible precursor to Dove's Blood Ink.

While reading through the book *Ancient Christian Magic,*[21] I discovered what could be a coherent precursor to modern Dove's blood ink from early common era Egypt: An incense formula against the powers of evil: "Draw the four angels in front of the curtain of the father, while you are wearing a wreath of roses, with a branch of myrtle in your hand and with gum ammoniac in your mouth. Offering; frankincense; storax; stacte (myrrh?) Slay the six doves. Cinnamon; rose oil…"[22]

Since the book *Ancient Christian Magic,* with formulas translated and published long after Slater's formula book, it makes one wonder if there is a hidden mystical connection between the two recipes. Even the celestial David Bowie comes into the history of using Dove's Blood Ink though the recipe doesn't include dragon's blood resin, probably a red dye was substituted instead; perhaps without coincidence, this is the earliest reference to this ink in modern times that I have found:

> *"Cherry recalled Bowie talking about a secretive group of magicians whom he believed were intent on harming him; on one occasion, biographers Tony Zanetta and Henry Edwards relate, he held a ritual to deflect the harmful spells directed at him. This entailed writing down the name of his magical nemesis and burning it at midnight, but when he missed the appointed time he was forced to perform a longer variant.*

---

[21] Meyer.

[22] ibid, 134.

> *This involved writing out the name using a special quill dipped in "dove's blood ink," a concoction containing cinnamon, bay leaves, alcohol, gum Arabic, and rose oil. After this, the piece of paper was folded in a prescribed manner and then burned."*[23]

What is a practitioner to do if they are needing to make these dragon's blood resin inks? Going back to my collection of old chemistry and manufacturing books, I discovered a little secret concerning dragon's blood resin. This I found in Roger's *Elements of Industrial Chemistry* from 1926: "Dragon's blood is odorless, tasteless, insoluble in water, but soluble in alcohol and ether, also soluble in the volatile and fixed oils, forming red solutions. Its principal use is in the coloring of varnish."[24] Here it would seem to be the solution to making an ink from dragon's blood resin. It satisfies the requirement of legibility and the formula preserves the crimson color. After a little experimentation, I came up with two possible recipes that I'm still at this time working to modify.

A Possible Working Dragon's Blood Ink, Two versions

First, to 1 gram of dragon's blood resin (Draco Cinnabari), add 100 drops of cinnamon oil. This should dissolve the resin and create an ink that flows from a dip pen but bleeds into paper. Secondly, to firm up the ink for more legible writing that doesn't bleed, make a copal resin varnish. This is made by taking 1 gram of clear copal resin and adding cinnamon oil

---

[23] White.

[24] Rogers, 455.

until the copal is dissolved. Then add to the dragon's blood resin ink the copal varnish, drop by drop until the ink is at the right viscosity. The amount of copal varnish added should be 15 to 20 drops. keep in an airtight jar and add a little more cinnamon oil if it starts to harden. The cinnamon oil should be anti-fungal enough to prevent mold.

Dragon's Blood Ink, Improved, version one

dragon's blood resin	*1 gram*
cinnamon oil	*100 drops*
copal varnish	*15 to 20 drops*

An improved version that I just discovered before this publication, makes an even more satisfying dragon's blood ink: The proportions are still being worked out but with a little bit of experiment, the curious ink-maker will find what works for them. Start off by taking a gram of crystal camphor and saturate it with about 2 ml or more of alcohol until all the camphor is dissolved. Then in this solution dissolve the dragon's blood resin. Then take the camphor solution and separately dissolve the copal resin, then add a little of the copal varnish to the dragon's blood resin solution until you achieve the right viscosity for writing with a pen. This ink has remained in solution for over a year now and has retained its intense crimson color; if after a time it thickens too much, you can always add more camphor-alcohol solution. After gleaning old industrial chemistry books, I discovered the key to dissolving resins such as dragon's blood resin and copal resin were the two ingredients of essential oils or camphor-alcohol solution.

Dragon's Blood Ink, Improved, version two

camphor resin	*1 gram*
alcohol	*2 ml, or as needed*
dragon's blood resin	*1 gram*
copal varnish, liquid	*as needed*

Perhaps we can be grateful for the work Slater had started, but there's no reason to blindly follow Slater's recipes. We can take our knowledge of herbs, animals, and minerals as inclusions and create our own recipes without being trapped in the wastelands of past formulas. One breakaway internet practitioner writes of their inclusions "For the Doves blood I added, burned doves feathers, cloves, dragons blood, hibiscus, cassia, gardenia, musk oil, damiana, gum arabic, and several other ingredients which will remain a secret!"[25]

Pacts with the Devil Ink

A recurring theme in pacts with the Devil is signing a book or legal document with one's own blood. The book, of course, is the Devil's analog to the bible. In history, Christianity developed dualistic parallels of symmetry in its theology as regards to Good and Evil. An example of this parallel is a Devil's Bible and autograph book as opposed to the Christian

[25] Avalon.

Bible and the Book of Life. Christopher Trigg[26] offers a fascinating account of the use of "spectral books" when those accused of witchcraft in colonial Salem Massachusetts in 1692, were impelled to sign their souls away to the Devil. The Devil's book, which always appeared to be different according to those accused, was signed in one's own blood, or some other's blood from an inkwell or merely pointing a finger and touching the book. The discrepancies of the acts lead the accusers to believe that the books and blood inks were spectral, but binding nonetheless.

Pacts with spirits and the Devil were popularized by the Faust legends. In Goethe's *Faust*,[27] Mephistopheles states that "Blood is a quite special fluid," and "Any bit of paper's just as good. And you can sign it with a drop of blood." However, Marlowe's *Doctor Faustus*[28] relates a certain problem as Mephistopheles states, "But now thou must bequeath it solemnly, And write a deed of gift with thine own blood; For that security craves Lucifer." Faustus replies, "[Writing] Ay, so I do. But, Mephistophilis, My blood congeals, and I can write no more."

It would seem that blood is sticky messy stuff. A.E. Waite in *The Book of Ceremonial Magic*[29] offers an authentic magic ink recipe from c.15 century for making pact with spirits and the Devil:

> *"It is understood that the signature is written with the blood of the operator, but the deed itself requires a special preparation, as follows: Place river-water in a new, varnished earthenware pot, together with the powder hereinafter*

---

[26] Trigg.

[27] Johann Goethe, *Faust.*

[28] Christopher Marlowe, *Doctor Faustus.*

[29] Waite.

described. Then take sprigs of fern gathered on the Eve of St. John and vine twigs cut in the full moon of March. Kindle this wood by means of virgin paper, and when the water boils the ink will be made. It must be changed each time that there is occasion to write, that is to say, whensoever the appellation of a spirit is undertaken.

Power for Pact-Ink

Gall nut	*10 oz*
Roman Vitriol or Green Copperas	*3 oz*
Rock Alum or Gum Arabic	*3 oz*

Make an impalpable powder, and when you would compose the ink, use as described above."

This makes a rather good black ink recipe but there is a little confusion about the alum and the gum arabic, both of these ingredients should be used, as alum was a common additive in early modern inks reflecting its parallel use in the textile industry for fixing a dye to cloth or in this instance, fixing the ink to paper and preserving the color. The gum arabic is necessary for the ink to flow correctly from the pen and stick to the paper; so I have included both in my formulation:

Pact with the Devil Ink, New Formulation

Water	*400 ml*
oak galls, ground	*60 grams*
iron sulphate	*18 grams*

alum	*18 grams*
gum arabic	*18 grams*
clove oil	*a few drops*

Bring the ingredients oak galls, iron sulphate, and alum to a boil and reduce the liquid to 200 milliliters. Strain the liquid mixture through a filter. Then add the gum arabic in liquid form and the clove oil. Bottle air tight.

Ancient Egyptian Inks

In my research I have identified over a hundred and forty magical ink recipes. Twenty-six are for Ancient Egyptian magical inks. These mostly derive from the Greek Magical Papyri (PGM) and the book "Ancient Christian Magic," however, it's not from these original sources that these internet formulas derive. These recipes are filtered from popular books on Egyptian style magic and are modernized to the point of missing the original intent of the recipes. One such popular magic ink suggested on the internet is for a Besa's Magic Ink. Even though the formula is given with the original ingredients of crow and dove blood, it also includes a base of black writing ink, myrrh, cinnabar, mulberry sap, vetch, and wormwood. However, what the internet nor the popular books do not tell you, is this recipe is for receiving dreams from the African dwarf god, Bes, not for general magic workings.[30] This also applies to the edgy sounding Typhonian Ink recipe,[31] where in reality, the god Typhon was not the scary antinomian god that modern magicians would

---

[30] Betz, *PGM VIII*, 64-110.

[31] ibid., *PGM XII*, 96-106.

have us believe: the purpose of this Typhonian Ink was for magic business workings.

The most significant ink formula in the PGM would have to be the Magical Friendship Ink[32]:

Magical Friendship Ink

oak galls	*3 parts*
blue vitriol	*2 parts*
truffle	*4 parts*
myrrh	*1 part*
gum arabic	*3 parts*

Scholars and popular writers have missed that this is perhaps the earliest known oak gall ink recipe. Blue vitriol or copper sulphate is used other than the typical iron sulphate. The surprising ingredient in this recipe is the inclusion of truffle, which has a worldwide distribution and is still a cherished food source for nomadic tribes in North Africa and the Near East. It would appear to be a food of hospitality, today as well in ancient times.

One PGM ink that escaped the attention of popular writers of ancient Egyptian magic is:

Pitys' Ink for Questioning Corpses

red ochre

burnt myrrh

---

[32] ibid., PGM XII, 397-400.

Wormwood juice

evergreen juice

On a flax leaf write out AZEL BALEMACHO with the ink and put it in the mouth of the corpse. It is assumed this is all that is needed for a corpse to answer your questions.[33]

The most poignant point about these ancient Egyptian formulas is so few survive into modern times, that it's a temptation to view these inks for general purpose.

Saffron Inks

Another modern source for magical inks comes from the popular writer on Wicca, Scott Cunningham. Even though many people may dismiss his writings as light weight and casual style in his book, *The Complete Book of Incense, Oils & Brews* offers a first and rather good introduction to the making of magical inks with formulas. This also seems to be the first mention of magical inks using saffron which came to be known as "butterfly blood inks." Saffron has been used for coloring since ancient times and is frequently found in medieval Persian and Arab formularies. Cunningham gives a very brief description of this ink as:

"Magic Saffron Ink - Saffron essence makes a fine magical ink, but the price is exorbitant."[34]

Even though Cunningham says that the price is exorbitant, he offers no recipe, in truth, the cost of making this

---

[33] ibid., PGM IV, 2140-44

[34] Cunningham.

ink is well below the price of purchasing a bottle of commercial writing ink. One gram of saffron to make a half liter of this ink is about $5. The various recipes on the internet that have expanded from Cunningham's offering suggests using alcohol or water as the liquid base, I however find that water draws the yellow color from the saffron better than alcohol. Also, none of the internet recipes add alum, which I find critical to enhancing and preserving the color. Here is my formulation:

Saffron Ink Improved

Saffron	*1 gram*
Water	*0.5 liter*
Alum	*1 gram*
Gum Arabic	*sufficient for writing.*
Clove oil	*a few drops*

If one were to make a true Butterfly's Blood Ink, perhaps adding an actual butterfly preserved in alcohol afterwards to an ink bottle filled with saffron ink would be impressive.

Magical Inclusions

As I discussed with the saffron ink, it is possible and desirable to add inclusions into your ink formulas, as herbs, minerals, animal parts, etc. Having these inclusions, formulated to your tradition, serve to further enhance your magical ink. One anonymous source makes a spider ink that includes various tree barks, myrrh and frankincense, although how these are cooked up is not given, but suggest further possible explorations into the magical realm of ink making.

A Good Basic Black Ink

Here is one of my favorite black ink recipes that can be used for magical or mundane purposes; it's easy to make and writes in a very satisfactory way. There's something magical about the way the oak galls when mixed with the iron salt solution, turns into an intense black. There is also the inclusion of cloves and indigo. Generally, start with twice the amount of water the recipe requires. Grind up the oak galls to a fine powder and boil together with the iron sulphate for 15 to 30 minutes, strain and then add the sugar, cloves, indigo solution, and gum arabic. Bottle tightly and this should last for several years. The magic can begin when you decide what magical inclusions to add and when to perform the making, according to your tradition.

A very good writing ink from the early 1800s.[35]

> *"This recipe for ink was penned with a quill in a notebook kept from the 1830's and 1840's that also included instructions for making gunpowder. The page is headed "Useful Receipts." The recipe reads: "To make Black Ink - 1 1/2 oz. Galls; 1 oz. Gum Arabic; 1 oz. Sugr [sic] Candy; 1 1/2 oz. Copperas; 6 cloves; 1 Drm indigo; Infuse these in a Jug with 3 pints Boilg [sic] Water for 12 Hours stirring it occasionally." The sugar candy would make the ink glossy, the cloves would prevent molding, and the*

[35] Nickel, 37.

indigo was a provisional colorant.

Water, 3 pints	*1000 ml*	*200 ml*
Oak Galls, 1.5 oz.	*30 grams*	*6 grams*
Gum Arabic, 1 oz.	*20 grams*	*4 grams*
Sugar, 1 oz.	*20 grams*	*4 grams*
Iron Sulphate, 1.5 oz.	*30 grams*	*6 grams*
Cloves, 6 each	*4 each*	*1 or more*
Indigo, soluble, 1 dram	*1.25 grams*	*0.25 grams*

Conclusion

The making of magical inks and their formulations is so complex that it could take several books to properly write about this subject. What I have included is merely a brief overall survey, and clearly there is much more to research and explore. The magical practitioner should make these inks themselves for their specific needs and not be confined in the wasteland of bad recipes and misinformation without sources: in all, to make magical inks that will perfect their magically intentioned workings.

Bibliography

Alvarado, Denise. *The Voodoo Hoodoo Spellbook* (New York: Weiser 2011).

Avalon, Annwyn. *Water Witch Magical Inks!* (2012), accessed

https://www.patheos.com/blogs/waterwitch/2012/07/magickal-inks-there-are-always.html

Balfour-Paul, Jenny. *Indigo: Egyptian Mummies to Blue Jeans* (London: The British Museum Press 2016).

Betz, Hans Dieter. *The Greek Magical Papyri in Translation* (Chicago: University of Chicago Press 1992).

Carvalho, David N. *Forty Centuries of Ink, or a Chronological Narrative Concerning Ink and Its Background* (New York: Banks Law Publishing Co. 1904).

De Claremont, Lewis. *Legends of Incense, Herb, and Oil Magic,* Catherine Yronwode, ed. (1936; Forestville CA: Lucky Mojo Curio Co. 2016).

Cunningham, Scott. *The Magic of Incense, Oils & Brews: A Guide to their Preparation and Use* (St.Paul: Minnesota: Llewellyn Publishing 1986).

Helman-Ważny, Agnieszka. *The Archaeology of Tibetan Books.* (Leiden: Brill 2014).

Hopkins, Albert A. *The Scientific American Cyclopedia of Receipts, Notes and Queries* (New York: Munn & Co.1892).

Hoskins, Janet. "The Menstrual Hut and the Witch's Lair in Two Eastern Indonesian Societies." *Ethnology,* vol. 41, no. 4, 2002, 317–333.

Kieschnick, John. "Blood Writing in Chinese Buddhism." *Journal of the International Association of Buddhist Studies,* Volume 23, Number 2, 2000.

Kirani. *The Magick of Kirani and Harpocration* (London: 1685).

Meyer, Marvin & Smith, Richard. *Ancient Christian Magic* (Princeton University Press, 1999).

Nickell, Joe. *Pen, Ink, & Evidence* (Lexington, Kentucky: University Press of Kentucky 1990).

Rodgers, Charlotte. *The Bloody Sacrifice: A personal Experience of Contemporary blood rites* (UK: Mandrake of Oxford 2011).

Rogers, Allen. *Elements of Industrial Chemistry* (New York: D. Van Nostrand Co. 1926).

Slater, Herman. *Magickal Formulary Spellbook, Book 1* (New York: Magickal Childe 1981)

Sorceress Cagliastro. *Blood Sorcery Bible: Volume 1: Rituals in Necromancy.* (Tempe Arizona: The Original Falcon Press 2011).

Trigg, Christopher. "The Devil's Book at Salem." *Early American Literature,* vol. 49, no. 1, 2014, pp. 37–65.

Trinquier, Jean. "Cinnabaris et Sang-Dragon: Le cinabre, des anciens entre mineral, vegetal et animal" *Revue Archéologique,* Nouvelle Série, Fasc. 2, Presses Universitaires de France, 2013.

Waite, A.E. *The Book of Ceremonial Magick* (New York: Bell Publishing Co. 1969).

White, Ethan Doyle. "One Magical Movement from Kether to Malkuth: Occultism in the Work of David Bowie." *Correspondences 7,* no. 2 (2019) 1-43.

Two Sticks And A Gold Ring
The use of plants in Northern Italy folk magic

Giulia Turolla

To the ancestors that kept the fires alive,

To the plants and the spirits that taught them,

And to Charme, for her support and friendship.

"With all you potent herbs do I now intercede

and to your majesty make my appeal

ye were engendered by Mother Earth,

and given for a gift to all."

(Precatio omnium herbarum; VI CE)

When I was a child, Autumn was the season of horse chestnuts. We call them "castagne matte" (crazy chestnuts) and I thought they were wonderful, popping out from their green fleshy pods with such a smooth, shiny texture. They could be found in every park, next to the swings and the slides: round and clean, they made for much superior missiles than lumps of dirt, and the name hinted at something dangerous and slightly funny. So, we gleefully played little foragers, while sharpening our ballistic skills.

I remember one day I found one with an especially weird shape and, while I was studying it with all the fascination we strive so hard to regain as adults, my grandmother came to me and said: "This one, you should keep. Put it in your pocket and keep it there all winter: it will protect you from colds". Oral traditions are so resilient and, at the same time, so fragile.

I kept a strange chestnut in my pocket, one winter after the other, and then came adolescence and adulthood, and soon I forgot all about it. This tiny piece of magic was lost to me, until I read about it in an old book about local traditions prodded my memory. It all came back, along with a sense of wonderment at how easily we let pieces of folk culture slip by. How much have we lost, already?

This feeling of impermanence, this fear of time advancing and crumbling knowledge lovingly passed on for centuries, through the power given to it by our indifference and inability to listen to our elders, is what prompted me to take an interest in the folk magic traditions of the land where I live and where my ancestors have lived before me.

The Practice of *Segnature*

In many areas of Italy, especially in rural regions, folk healers are still present and active. Their legacy, though, is rapidly fading, with the advancement of modern medicine, rising mistrust and cynicism towards traditional methods and the increasing difficulty in finding people that meet the criteria that are required to receive "the gift" (or, failing that, that are simply interested enough and willing to learn). Even if many common elements and themes can be traced throughout the peninsula, there are marked differences between northern and southern traditions as, for example, the greater focus on fascination and the evil eye that can be observed in the regions of the South. While moving North, the practices that receive more attention are mostly oriented at healing specific illnesses or conditions that are the result of more mundane reasons. My research focuses on Northern Italy and, with special attention to the region Emilia Romagna where I, and the people that passed on this practice to me, live.[1]

"*Segnature*" can be loosely translated as "signatures" and the meaning of the word resides in the gesture of making signs. Non-Italian people, when hearing about signatures, will probably think about Paracelsus' doctrine of signatures[2] (and, as we will see, there is a relationship between this theory and *segnature*). While in Italy Paracelsus and his theories are known only by a limited amount of people and the vast majority of people know *segnature* only as a folk healing practice, with these core features:

- It is performed through the use of signs (symbols traced with hands and fingers, simple ritualized procedures that can involve herbs, oil, water and other objects of common use) and the uttering of secret formulas.
- Only the people that have received the gift of *segnature* from someone else can learn the formulas and perform the practices. There are usually precise signs indicating who should receive this gift.

[1] Northern Italy is a more complex area to investigate when it comes to folk magical practices. It's the richest and more developed part of the country. People are less likely to openly talk about folk magic, because it's socially perceived as being the result of ignorance and superstition (which doesn't stop them from availing themselves of these practices in private). As the majority of XIX century Italian migrants in the USA were from southern regions, this affects the way in which Italian folk magic is known and represented across the ocean.

[2] A theory later expanded and spread by the works of Giambattista della Porta and Jakob Böhme, whose main characteristic was the belief that plants showing resemblances with specific parts of the body or ailments, carry the properties needed to cure them.

- The gift has to be passed on the night of the 24th of December. The transmission must happen orally and is sometimes preceded by fasting. In some cases formulas have to be repeated on this night, every year (even if no transmission is being performed) to keep their power alive and strong.
- There is not a single magical act that can cure everything: the single traditional practices are linked to specific illnesses and conditions.
- The practices are most frequently addressed at physical ailments, such as Herpes Zoster (*Fuoco di Sant'Antonio*),[3] warts, back pain, sciatica, styes, sprains, athrepsia[4], burns, headaches etc...However the ailments can also be of a psychological/emotional nature (fears/phobias, depression) and/or of a spiritual/magical one (the evil eye, the "fallen soul").[5] Finally the ailments can also have a mixed nature, such as it can be observed most eloquently in the case of worms.
- The healers should not ask a fee in exchange for their services, but can accept gifts.
- Healing is often performed at dawn and on an empty stomach.

---

[3] Herpes Zoster, in particular, is strictly linked with *segnature*: so much so, that even in the most economically developed areas of northern Italy it's still possible to find a medical doctor advising his/her patients to seek a traditional healer for this illness, as the most efficient and permanent cure to be had.

[4] A newborn illness caused by malnutrition that was once relatively common.

[5] *Anima caduta* ("fallen soul") is a condition remarkably similar to what many indigenous cultures would call a fragmented or damaged soul. The overall condition of the person showing signs of depression, reduced energies and zest for life are thought to be caused by the soul falling lower than its proper place in the body.

- Frequently the use of a gold ring is required to perform many kinds of *segnature*. It's usually a wedding band, but there are conflicting versions on the fact that it should be the healers very wedding band as opposed to another one that was passed on to him/her.

Traditions can show small variations from area to area (or, sometimes, even from home to home), but these main features can usually be found in every genuine manifestation of this kind.

The Transmission of the Gift

Modern times can be hard on traditional healers looking for a successor, especially if you are supposed to find someone that is the seventh child of a seventh child (with an uninterrupted line of either all-male or all-female children), as one of the most widespread versions of the tradition recommendations. Just a couple of generations ago, it was relatively common, especially in rural settings, to find families with a dozen or more children, so finding the seventh child of a seventh child was a demanding, but not impossible, task. Currently, the fertility rate in my country has dropped to 1.3 children per woman and finding such a specimen is the equivalent of winning a hefty sum at the lottery. Folk healers have been forced to adapt to a rapidly changing social, cultural and economic situation. Some of them have reacted by deciding that keeping the tradition alive is more important than honoring what they have been taught to the letter. Others seem to have surrendered to modernity, reasoning that the time for these practices is past and that there is no point in trying to preserve them further.

Being a seventh child of a seventh child is far from

being the only special mark indicating who should receive the gift of *segnature*. Here are some of the most frequent variants:

- Being born with a caul
- Being born a *settimino/a* (a preterm baby, born on the seventh month of gestation)
- Being a woman who gave birth to twins (preferably non-identical ones: a male and a female)
- Being a blood relative of the person passing on the gift (usually a daughter/son, or a niece)

In some cases there's also the belief that, in order to receive the *segnature* later on in life, the relatives need to place a specific object either in the hands of the newborn, right after birth, or to abscond it in his/her bindings while baptism is administered. The kind of object is directly related to the type of illness the baby will be able to cure as an adult: a contorted vine for sprains, wheat/rice kernels for warts, an extinguished ember (or a burning vine stick if it was placed in the hand) for burns, flowers for eye illnesses, a silkworm for worms, and needle and thread for styes.[6]

In one case I have encountered, the rule that the healer should receive *segnature* three times, before being able to pass them on to someone else. This case presented other anomalies.[7] I am personally inclined to believe this was not a widespread notion, but the fact that the secret formulas should have been repeated every Christmas Eve to reinforce their power can be found in many instances.

Currently, most healers are passing down *segnature* to people chosen among their friends and relatives that show a

---

[6] This use seems to be particularly rooted in Romagna, see Giovetti Paola, 2016.

[7] See note 10.

marked interest and a predisposition both to the practice and to healing as a selfless act of service to the community; the practitioners are mostly women. This should not come as a surprise, given the tie this tradition has with the space of the home and especially the kitchen, although men are not excluded from learning. Being deeply religious is not an absolute requirement[8], but having faith in the healing power of *segnature* is, as most healers agree, the firm belief of the person performing the practice to be an essential ingredient for its efficacy. Most sources agree that the secret formulas should be learned by heart and, most importantly, need to be transmitted orally and recited in their entirety for the benefit of those receiving the gift. Many people these days write them down and take care to keep them safe from prying eyes.

24th

Christmas Eve is the right time to pass on *segnature.*[9] This tradition goes back at least half a millennium ago[10] and, as it

[8] Most people of advanced age in Italy show at least a perfunctory attachment to the Catholic faith, but, at least in the areas I'm focusing on, this is not an aspect that receives particular attention: many formulas (often the ones that sound more ancient) show no ties to Catholicism and, even when saints/Jesus or Mary are present, it seems like their names are simply an addition to empower the formula, root it in Christianity (thus relieving the mind of the catholic healer, that would be horrified at being called a witch) and provide an acceptable reason for its efficacy.

[9] I have only encountered a single case, so far, in which the people passing on segnature advised June 24th as an additional date for the transmission: since the people in question were quite young (in respect to the elders that usually fulfill this role) and showed an interest in magical traditions and folklore as a whole, the person that received *segnature* from them and I agree in thinking it an attempt to flesh out the bare bones that have been preserved by adding bits and pieces retrieved in folk culture (the 24th of June is an important magical night in Italian traditions, mostly known for the making of S. John's Water).

[10] See the testimony of a healer in Milani Marisa, 2016.

can be expected, most healers believe this fact to be directly connected to the event of Jesus birth,[11] although this predilection shows roots that precede Christianity.

From *Lectisternium Telluri,* to the Saturnalia, the Roman calendar reveals how the second half of December and the first days of January were mostly dedicated to chthonic deities and spirits.[12] As the seeds were resting in the hard, cold soil, chthonic deities and spirits were called upon to protect them in that delicate phase in which life was surrounded by darkness and asked to ensure a fruitful harvest in the following months.

During the time between the end of the old year and the beginning of a new one, vegetation falls in a deep sleep. The green of life withers and survival becomes harder for plants, animals and humans alike. As the light is at its minimum, other creatures that usually reside in darkness and in the depths of the earth, appear to roam the realm of the living. The same phenomenon can be observed in the tradition of Halloween, with its Celtic roots firmly grounded in what was the end of the agricultural year. The liminal time between the death of the old and the birth of the new, in both cases, is the moment in which spirits of the dead and other creatures of darkness rise from their normal dwelling place. It is no wonder that these festivities share many focal traits, as children going door to door in search of gifts and sweetmeats, the caveats about the possibility of witches, werewolves and similar creatures manifesting in particular places like crossroads, cemeteries, etc... and the act of donning monstrous costumes. Last but not least, comes the old custom of preparing a feast for the dead, so that loved ones and

---

[11] See note 9.

[12] 13th of December: Lectisternium Telluri (dedicated to Tellus and Ceres); 15th: Consualia (dedicated to Consus, god of wheat kernels); 17th-23rd: Saturnalia (dedicated to Saturn).

ancestors can share the food of the living once again.

This particular gesture in the Christmas period often takes the form of the European tradition of the Yule log. All over Italy, until World War II, many variations of this theme could be observed, where a big log was placed in the hearth on Christmas Eve and libations were poured on it.[13] This gesture meant to free the spirits of the dead,[14] later took on a meaning centered on keeping newborn Jesus, Mary, Joseph, and the three Mages (depending on local versions) warm during the night.

Taking care of the spirits of the dead served a double purpose, since on the one hand it meant courting their support and goodwill in helping the agricultural process, as chthonic beings, they could oversee and exercise power upon. On the other hand, it was meant to appease them and avoid the potential harm that was inherent in their ambivalent nature.

It is certainly significant how a practice skating on the thin edge between respectability and heresy, piety and magic, is so tightly connected to a day that seems to share in its ambiguity. As it can be expected, most of the healers performing *segnature* choose to believe that Christmas Eve is chosen because of its significance as the night of Jesus' birth, as it has been established in Christianity. However, looking at local folklore, it's impossible to miss how this night was reputed to have a special significance for witches.[15] I tend to believe that the importance of this date in the transmission of the gift, stems in part from the

---

[13] See Baldini Eraldo, Bellosi Giuseppe, 2012.

[14] This was not the only symbolic and ritual meaning of the Yule log: other themes are certainly present, such as the necessity of keeping the light alive during the solstitial critical passage.

[15] On this night (and, sometimes, the ones immediately before and after it) witches could be seen gathering, especially at crossroads. They were thought to be particularly active and to share the secrets of their art with one another. (See note n 14).

necessity of transmitting a magical power that was not openly recognized as such. The passage from one being to another was made easier and possible in the suspended time between the stillness of death and rebirth and at the same time, from the role that ancestral power and lineage have in the bestowing and preservation of the gift.

The Green Beast: Humans Interaction with the Vegetal Realm

As people born in this century, in cultures characterized by monotheistic faiths, as well as anthropocentrism and consumerism, we are used to the idea of plants as no more than elements in a scenery. One of the most striking consequences of devoting oneself to studying and listening to our vegetal brethren, is how their individual nature starts emerging from the green mass surrounding us. Something that seemed so homogenous and motionless suddenly starts breathing and moving. The same plants haunt and follow us wherever we go. Stepping into a forest is no longer just a journey in a pleasant landscape hoping for a glimpse of wild fauna, but a veritable immersion in a living net of symbols, a complex melody of differences, interrelations and personalities.

No more than a century ago, the green world was still, especially for the lower classes, a living creature, composed of individual names, stories, and gifts. The garden was as much of a resource as the woods and the bogs, where places in which the potential for life and death could be harvested. Making use of plants and other remedies involved the assumption of a point of view that was very different from the one we are used to. Humans, plants, animals, minerals and every phenomenon material and natural are all bound in a common web of symbols and meaning that have a circular and potentially infinite nature.[16]

In Renaissance's episteme,[17] memory was perceived to be a divine instrument. The tool with which it was possible to plumb the depths of the complex tangle of sympathies, antipathies and similarities and find the thread, relationship, and story that could bring forth the knowledge needed to face the specific issue at hand. Cabinet of curiosities[18] were not merely a divertissement, but real knowledge machines. Standing into a place where all the primary elements and parts of the cosmos were represented, it was possible to grasp all the connections that went unseen in a day-by-day existence, and get closer to God's own understanding of the world.

The influence of this worldview affected the noble and cultured classes, but also ignorant peasants, and every strata in between, and its effects lingered. In fact, much longer in folk culture than in so-called "higher" contexts, where it was mostly blown away first by Enlightenment and then by its sterner child, Positivism. The vast reservoir of knowledge painstakingly collected and transmitted in rural areas, the tales about plants that cure and plants that kill, were submitted to a gradual process of Christianization. It came to pass that the power of green beings was, at the same time, domesticated and purified by gaining a connection to saints that was highlighted with the adoption of names and the spreading of etiological stories.

The disquieting, ineffable power of the great green beast, with all its children, became the reflection of the

---

[16] The very same that originated the concept of magical correspondences as we know them.

[17] The way in which knowledge is organized and structured.

[18] The first one was born in Florence in a period between 1444 and 1492 by Lorenzo il Magnifico and is considered to be the first museum of Europe.

iridescent wave of the Cosmos and an expression of God's might.[19] In the same way, village healers were able to keep their traditions alive and their sense of self-worth intact. They were not witches or sorcerers handling suspicious powers, but people of faith healing through creatures blessed by the Saints and God's own magnificence.

Witches, Healers, and Shamans

The discussion of shamans is quite prolific in the last fifty years. It is therefore next to impossible to avoid including shamanism in a discourse regarding folk healing practices transmitted in an initiatory manner and performed through physical gestures. Keeping firmly in mind that shamanism, as a somewhat homogeneous and trans-cultural phenomenon, is a scholarly construct generated by anthropological and ethnographic studies,[20] as well as all the limits of the comparative method, it is possible to highlight the features that could bring the phenomenon of *segnature* at least partly under the umbrella of shamanic behavior. Several points include:

- As with most forms of shamanism, it is a set of practices primarily centered on healing and performed as a service to a community.
- Healers need to go through an initiatory ceremony in order to fully acquire their powers.

---

[19] Only a handful of plants, because of their manifestly "wicked" nature, could not be included in this operation. Thus, precisely as the devil and its minions lurk at the borders of Christianity, filling every void, the plants of the witches haunt gardens and wild places.

[20] Even in Siberia, where the term "shaman" originated, it's not possible to reduce shamanism into a clearly defined set of ritual behavior, social role, cosmology, technique etc…(See R. Hutton, 2001).

- The gift is either inherited through family lineage and / or is bestowed on someone showing specific signs. Sometimes the gift has to be passed on at the time of the healer's death.
- The act of healing is a performative one and not a static one and the formulas alone are not sufficient: the signs traced on and around the body, the instruments and objects used and the personal belief and the emotional, psychological and spiritual involvement of the healer have an equal, if not a greater, importance.
- A survey conducted on 200 informants showed how the majority (132) believed the healer to be in a non-ordinary state of consciousness during the healing ritual[21].
- In the province of Modena a big copper pan can be used in a way that is reminiscent of a shaman's drum, with the practitioner striking it with an open hand on its bottom; the pan is used only in these ritual occasions and is cared for in a special manner.[22]
- Signs are traced in the air and on the body of the patient, especially circles and crosses,[23] using

---

[21] Benozzo Francesco, 2008.

[22] ibid.

[23] Benozzo (Ibid.) highlights how tracing circles and crosses is a characteristic especially present in Siberian shamanisms; however it should be noted that perambulation and the tracing of a circle is one of the most widespread features of magical practices in different cultures and times. It's interesting to notice how the crosses traced in *segnature* (as well as those built with sticks and other objects) are usually of the equal arms kind and that, contrary to what could be expected, no emphasis is put on the relationship between these crosses and Jesus' cross.

hands or even metallic objects.[24]

- The act of healing often involves the idea of opening the body to extract the illness[25]. There is also often the transmission of the illness to something else, such as the gold ring,[26] stick crosses, and water or plants used by the practitioner. In one case we even have a testimony of a formula openly stating that the illness is being taken away by an animal spirit.[27]
- When plants are involved, it is often stressed the importance of harvesting them in wild nature, even when they are species commonly grown or cultivated in gardens. This is similar to the greater power accorded to wild plants and animal spirits in many forms of shamanism, as opposed to domesticated ones.
- Sometimes amulets are prepared as a number of ingredients and / or a formula written in a piece of paper, sewn into a square of cloth. The amulet has to be kept secret and should not be opened in order to preserve its power.[28]

The possible relationship between European witchcraft and shamanism have already been noticed and discussed at

---

[24] In the area of the Appennino in the region of Emilia Romagna, the use of the *manarino* (a sort of little one-handed axe) is particularly frequent.

[25] In the Modena province and surrounding areas, the *segnatura* is called *averta,* which can be roughly translated as "the opened" or "the opening."

[26] In this case the ring has to be put down on the floor, to discharge the illness into the earth.

[27] "*Lévra lévra ch at pàsa la févra la lévra la vóla la tórna pió sóla ed là da la lòuna la lévra la vóla" ("Hare hare may the fever go away, away the hare flies, comes back relieved and beyond the moon, the hare flies").* Formula published in F.Benozzo, 2008.

[28] Benozzo, 2008, Giovetti, 2016, and Giuseppe, 1981.

length by C. Ginzburg.[29] In this landscape *segnature* seem to represent a slice of folk magic that was able to avoid the massive repression and persecution faced by other kinds of witchcraft, probably because of its focus on healing, which made it more difficult to present it as a an evil practice. Its usefulness and ability to adapt and don a vest that is, at least on the surface, compatible with the Catholic faith. That's how it survived and how we are able to find some frayed threads, here and there, that speak to us of spirit helpers, and ecstasy and power transmissions in the heart of the darkest night.

The Kitchen as a Place of Power

In a not-so-distant past, food was far from being the safe, commonplace heaven we tend to take for granted. The *simplicia* employed to cure and cause diseases were, most often than not, the very same that figured in a day by day diet. There was no sharp divide between medicines/poisons and the ingredients that were harvested and transformed into food, as both came from the same places. The garden, forest, and the extraction of active principles of modern pharmacology were still evolving.

The idea that the food that people ingested could change their state of consciousness and affect their bodies (sometimes in a dramatic way) was well rooted in everyone's mind and taken as a simple fact of life. Our culture did not feature any particular taboo when it came to food, so in times of famine everything, including poisons and human flesh,[30] became fair game. However, even in normal times, lower classes routinely ingested bread adulterated with ryegrass,[31] as

---

[29] Ginzburg, 2004.

[30] Camporesi, Piero, 2002.

[31] *Lolium.*

the standards of food preparation were far from being at the level at which we are accustomed, especially for poor people, which caused a drunk-like attitude, like trance states and frenzy. Up until the XVII century it was considered normal to anoint oneself (or babies) with poppy laced ointments before going to bed, to prepare for the dream realm.

Cooking was a very close relative to Alchemy and the fires of the kitchen were the place where it took place the transformation of the *simplicia,* in their wild and natural state, into food fit for human consumption. The connection between what was harvested in nature and what ended up on the plate was, especially if compared to our current understanding, extremely strong and immediate: almost no processing took place outside of one's own kitchen, which became the literal space where materia and life turn into sustainment for other beings.

At the same time, the kitchen was where most of the healing activities of the medium to lower classes took place. For a long time, until the dawn of modern medicine, the remedies used by household women, barbers, midwives, and traveling surgeons were more effective than the treatments of a cultured medicine based more on philosophical abstractions, than on the study and observation of actual results. The kitchen was the place where the ingredients needed for these remedies were stored, where poultices and concoctions were prepared and the power of the plants and other *simplicia* was harnessed and directed towards the desired outcome. As Marcel Mauss observed,[32] the cauldron, the cooking pot, was the altar of the sorcerer.

For people of medium to low social class, the kitchen also represented the true core of the house, the space where all the family would get together, meet visiting outsiders and

---

[32] Mauss, Marcel, "A General Theory of Magic" (Routledge: 2008).

engage in social interaction. Italians, in particular, have been worshipping at the altar of the power of food for a very long time; as a social glue, as a medium of communication and exchange, as an embodiment of culture, ancestral traditions and ties to the land and all its inhabitants. Even today the kitchen keeps its special place as the heart of the house and the family, as formal meetings happen in the living room, but family and friends are welcomed in the warm embrace of the kitchen, with all its fragrant mysteries. It should therefore come as no surprise that the kitchen is still the very place in which the practice of *segnature* is usually performed. It is a space where women's power and rule was and largely still is unquestioned, where family recipes and secrets are passed on and tradition is honored and protected.

Plants of Healing and Power

The following is a brief description of the plants I have selected as seeming more tightly connected to the tradition of *segnature*. This list, that has no pretense of being all-comprehensive or even to accomplish the impossible feat of establishing a canon, takes into consideration three main aspects related to the plants: their presence in the praxis of *segnature*, the history and local folklore/customs connected to them,[33] and their status as a recognized *"Erba di San Giovanni"* (Saint John's Herb).[34]

[33] Further information on these subjects can be found, among others, in Cattabiani, Alfredo, 1996; Ungarelli Gaspare, 1921; Adani Giuseppe, Tamagnini Gastone, 1981; La Sorsa Saverio, 1941; Giannitrapani Mario, 2010.

[34] As previously stated, Saint John's night (the night between the 23th and the 24th of June) was considered, together with Christmas Eve, the most important moment of the year for witches, spirits and healing rituals alike. Saint John's Herbs were those herbs (roots, bulbs etc…) that had to be harvested on that particular night to reach

Saint John's wort *(Hypericum perforatum)*

It is considered THE Saint John's Herb par excellence and its popular name *"cacciadiavoli"* ("devils' bane") is a strong indicator of its apotropaic properties. Hypericum oil, with its bright red color, is one of the most widespread homemade remedies and its efficacy in treating burns cannot be overstated.[35]

After the end of the dances around the bonfires, on Saint John's night, small bundles of this plant were thrown on the roof of the houses, to protect them from lightning and evil spirits; for the same reasons it could be burned in the hearth or buried under the threshold. Its apotropaic powers made it a frequent presence in protective amulets and before or after healing treatments.

Olive (Olea europaea)

Olive branches are, without a doubt, the most frequently used plants in *segnature*. It is my personal opinion that in recent times, with the decrease of domestic foraging and the waning of folklore and tradition connected to the use of healing and magical plants, olive branches have gradually come to take the place that was once kept by other plants. The reason for this shift is simple enough. Thanks to Palm Sunday, every Catholic home, no matter its inhabitants' propensity towards harvesting wild herbs, has a bundle of blessed olive branches ready at hand[36]. *Segnature* are passed on orally, so it stands to

---

maximum efficacy.

[35] I have once personally witnessed how a swift application of this oil on a second degree burn (as an emergency measure while waiting for medical treatment) significantly decreased the pain in an incredibly short time.

[36] Every church on Palm Sunday mass, provides enough blessed olive branches for all

reason that, while knowledge and awareness about properties of plants were sliding into oblivion, people would find it made sense to use the one plant they always had in their possession that had an unquestionable power, especially since most were convinced that the force behind their healing skills stemmed from the same source that had blessed the branches.

The use of olive in Palm Sunday, instead of the palms that are mentioned in the biblical passage, is tied to a long standing Mediterranean tradition of this tree as a sacred one, that vastly predates Christianity.[37] In *segnature,* olive is used to avert evil, in the form of a sickness, an unwanted person or a storm. Furthermore, olive oil is well known for being the main medium to divine the presence of the evil eye (the detecting and averting of which is present in *segnature,* but in a marginal way).

Wheat and Barley (Triticum; Hordeum Vulgare)

Cereals, which are paramount to human survival in a sustenance-based agriculture, are the focus of many rituals and traditions all over the world. Numerous local variations feature the creation of a fetish often as the simple form of the last harvest or as a braided wheat doll, for the spirit of wheat to inhabit until the following harvest or just up to the sowing time, where its sacrifice would have infused life force in the seeds waiting to sprout. In *segnature* wheat and barley kernels are prominent in the healing of worms and warts. Once the healing ritual has been completed, the kernels are to be left

---

its parishioners to bring home. Traditionally the branches are kept in the house until new ones take their place, one year later.

[37] Olive was, of course, sacred to the goddess Athena, but also to Jove and Minerva. Branches of olive were brought in houses on the calends of January, to assure prosperity for the new year.

near a well or a ditch, and if someone picks them up or touches them, chances are that he/she will pick up the warts and worms, as well.[38]

Garlic (Allium Sativum)

Garlic has a well-known power of averting evil that has been passed on to popular culture thanks to its role in vampire tales, and like it often happens, garlic, with its chthonic nature, enjoys a deep connection to the same beings it is wont to protect from. In *segnature,* garlic sometimes appears with the healing of worms (and, in fact, it does have anthelmintic properties), but even more as an amulet. In this capacity, it had to be picked on S. John's night,[39] and kept in the home the whole year.

Fennel (Foeniculum vulgare)

Fennel's presence in *segnature* is very specifically tied to curing eye diseases,[40] and the reason for this can be identified quite easily, as Pliny the Elder states that in the Spring, snakes look for fennel to rub themselves on, in order to facilitate the shedding of their skin and to restore the sight that had dimmed during the winter months.[41] Ginzburg's *benandanti* (in north-east Italy) fought battles with witches, armed with

---

[38] Leavings from *segnature* are often to be left in places where they will rot quickly, thus dispersing the diseases attached to them. In this specific case, it is possible that the presence of water is meant to wash away the filth in a quicker way.

[39] Today many people simply resort to buying it on the same day.

[40] Other times eye diseases in *segnature* require the use of flowers of unspecified kind.

[41] This is a nice example of how the mutual exchange between "higher" and "lower" culture was more frequent and flowing than was previously thought.

fennel maces:[42] probably because, once again, its connection to snakes allowed it to exercise a special power on demonic beings.

Rue (Ruta graveolens)

Like Hypericum, Rue is another Saint John's herb with apotropaic properties that can be found in amulets, specifically the leaves on which butterflies had laid their eggs were particularly sought out and in simple gestures meant to remove and avert evil spirits. It was thought to repel snakes, a fact later confirmed by scientific observation, and this, coupled with its natural anthelmintic properties, goes well in hand with its principal role in *segnature,* as an ingredient in recipes and rituals meant to get rid of worms.

Mugwort (Artemisia vulgaris)

For centuries, people believed that on Saint John's night, mugwort would secrete a special lump of coal, that could be found digging underneath the roots, and could protect its owners from many dangers, including lightning, poisons, evil spirits… even plague itself. The precise nature of this coal has not been established, but a medicine text of the 18th century speculates that it was just a detached and dried out root piece.[43] Mugwort was used for prophetic purposes in healing: leaves were put under the pillow of the sick and if the person fell asleep right away it was a sign of impending recovery.

I have not personally found *segnature* where the use of mugwort was specifically mentioned, though I consider this to

---

[42] Ginzburg.

[43] Giuseppe, Antonelli, "Dizionario compendiato delle scienze mediche," vol.I, 154, 1827-30.

be is mostly due to the process I described in the paragraph about olive, but mugwort is mentioned in the late 16th century as being used to summon storms by tying it upside-down on a tree and to protect houses from evil magic, when affixed on the door.[44]

Rosemary (Rosmarinus officinale)

For a Mediterranean soul, Rosemary is much more than a popular seasoning or an effective officinal herb. From the roasts and baked potatoes that gather all the family around the table on lazy Sundays, to its ever-present plant curled up next to the doors and gates, rosemary smells like home. Rosemary's connection with the soul of the home must have been ancient and deep, as the Romans crowned the statuettes of the Lares with its branches. In the province of Bologna, it was said that when it was planted in the garden, if the plant successfully survived someone in the house was going to die.[45] In the same province, rosemary flowers are believed to bestow happiness when worn in contact with skin, while the leaves can avert nightmares and increase memory with their smell.

Rosemary is another one of those herbs that should be harvested on Saint John's night, but its flowering tops could also be picked on the first days of June, put in a light blue or light pink sachet to be burned on Saint John's fires, in order to get rid of bad influences and propagate good fortune.[46]

---

[44] Giovan Battista Codronchi, "De morbis veneficis ac veneficiis", chapter VIII, 1595.

[45] This suggests the idea of Rosemary as a familiar spirit, protecting the house and its inhabitants in exchange for a life.

[46] Elisabetta Martelli and Maria Teresa Zanetti, "Erbe magiche per piatti incantati" (Atesa: 2000), 116.

Vine (Vitis vinifera)

Vine, with its juicy grapes and hardy constitution, is the rich blood flowing from the Earth. It's Dionysus and his boisterous mysteries of death and rebirth and the ecstatic embrace of the Great Mother. In *segnature* vine branches are used in the healing of sprains, especially if they are twisted in a double spiral. They also appear in Romagna, where a vine branch on fire is to put in a newborn's hand to allow him/her to be able to heal burns, as an adult.

Fern (Dryopteris filix mas)

A tradition that is widespread in all of Europe, with local variants, connects this fern to Saint John's night, when its seeds should be picked in order to make use of their magical powers. In the area I'm taking into consideration, it was believed that the seeds appeared, matured, and fell to the ground, all on the same night. People looking for good fortune and abundance went traipsing in the forest at midnight, attempting to find the coveted seeds. Though it was used to kill tapeworm, I haven't found *segnature* mentioning fern in this specific capacity.

Bramble (Rubus ulmifolius)

With its sharp thorns and its disquieting tendency to grasp and devour any unattended place, the long standing association of bramble with pain, vice and other sinister emotions is a legacy that even its sweet berries cannot erase. Thus, it is no great surprise how this plant figures in *segnature* as connected to one of the most painful illnesses, one that gave no respite, St. Anthony's fire.

Fig (Ficus carica var. caprificus)

Everyone who ever picked a ripe fig knows the branches of this plant are supple. It is probably this characteristic that, in *segnature,* puts it into connection with sciatica and rheumatism. In some cases whole branches are used, and only the bark in others.

Thistle (gen. Carduus)

Thistle is yet another S. John's plant with apotropaic properties. Its flowers were used on that special night for love divinations[47] and were affixed on the doors of houses and stables to repel evil spirits.

Greek Mountain Tea (Sideritis Montana)

In the province of Bologna, this plant is commonly called *"erba de la pôra"* ("Herb of fear"), because of its role in a ritual meant to cure children of those fears that arise suddenly and without apparent cause. The plant is boiled and the child is washed in the resulting decoction, from head to feet. If the water comes away cloudy and with strange characteristics similar to shredded pieces of cloth, the operation is considered successful, otherwise it has to be repeated.

Wild Rose (Rosa canina)

Roses symbolically bloom in the plagues of saints and of Jesus himself and have a long standing association with the Virgin Mary, and before her, with many other goddesses. It was a

[47] The flowers are picked and slightly burned on the fire, before putting them in a glass with some water: if the flower revives, it means that love is returned.

special delight for me, to receive the gift of a *segnatura* that requires that one cut some hair on the 15th of august, the day of the assumption of the Virgin, and puts it on a branch of wild rose, in order to get rid of warts and, possibly, other skin afflictions.

Finally, our journey through the fascinating tradition of segnature, comes to its end, but is this an end or only a new beginning? Is this song of remembrance just a tale of times gone by or is it another spin of the wheel?

Every time I step into my garden, to tend the plants that have inhabited our traditions, cooking and healing practices for centuries, I hear the voices of my ancestors whispering to me and their hands guiding my gestures; my daughter already knows to look for a shiny "crazy chestnut" at the first stirrings of autumn and my little son greets the fairies every time we stroll next to the big Black Poplar, with its odorous buds. By passing on these traditions we take a chalice that has been handed to us and by reaching out to the spirits of these plants and working with them, we fill that chalice with new life, before sharing it with those that will come after us.

May the old ways always find open ears and kind hands, may the green spirits whisper our names in dark forests and dance with us in sunny fields.

"That I may ever be allowed

with the favor of your majesty

to gather you [...]

and I shall set forth the produce of the fields for you

and return thanksthrough the name of the

Mother who ordained your birth."

(Precatio omnium herbarum; VI CE)

Bibliography

Adani, Giuseppe e Tamagnini Gastone (a cura di); AA. VV. "Cultura popolare nell'Emilia Romagna – Medicina, Erbe e Magia," Federazione delle Casse di Risparmio e delle Banche del Monte dell'Emilia e della Romagna, 1981.

Baldini Eraldo, Bellosi Giuseppe. "Tenebroso Natale. Il lato oscuro della grande festa," Laterza, 2012.

Benozzo Francesco. "Lepri che volano, carri miracolosi, padelle come tamburi: una tradizione etnolinguistica preistorica in area emiliana," Quaderni di semantica, 2008.

Camporesi, Piero. "Il pane selvaggio," Bompiani, 2016.

Cattabiani, Alfredo. "Lunario," Mondadori, 2011.

Cattabiani, Alfredo. "Florario," Mondadori, 1997.

Eliade, Mircea. "Lo Sciamanismo e le tecniche dell'estasi," Edizioni Mediterranee, 2005.

La Sorsa, Saverio. "Alberi, piante ed erbe medicinali nella tradizione popolare italiana," pp. 99-129, Lares Vol. 12, No. 2 , Aprile 1941.

Giannitrapani, Mario. "Ierobotanica, un'Ecologia Preistorica del Sacro," Simmetria, 2010.

Ginzburg, Carlo. "Ecstasies: deciphering the Witches' Sabbat," University of Chicago, 2004.

Ginzburg, Carlo. "The Night Battles: Witchcraft and Agrarian Cults in the Sixteenth and Seventeenth centuries," Routledge, 2012.

Giovetti, Paola. "I guaritori di campagna," Mediterranee, 2016.

Hutton, Ronald. "Shamans. Siberian Spirituality and the Western Imagination," Hambledon Continuum, 2007.

Milani, Marisa. "Streghe, morti ed esseri fantastici nel Veneto," Esedra, 2016.

Ungarelli, Gaspare. "Le piante aromatiche e medicinali nei nomi e nell'uso della tradizione popolare bolognese", Tipografia L. Parma, 192

14
LA MUERTE

The Garden of Death
An Herbal Lore of la Santisima Muerte

Jesse Hathaway Diaz

One does not live forever on this earth:

We endure only for an instant!

Will flowers be carried to the Kingdom of Death:

Is it true that we are going?...

Thy heart knows:

Just once do we live!...

Here, among flowers that enclose us,

among flowery boughs you are singing!

-Nezahualcoyotl , 15th Century King of the City State of Texcoco (Pre-Conquest Mexico)

Santa Muerte de mi corazón, no me desampares de tu protección.

Holy Death, near to my heart, do not leave me

without your protection.

-Traditional Prayer for la Santisima Muerte

Who is *la Muerte*? or, Death as told by plants as told by *un pocho*

An inheritance of Spanish Roman Catholicism and indigenous belief and respect for death, *la Santa Muerte,* the Mexican folk saint of Death, is approachable by everyone, for She has seen all, just as She levels all. Patron of the home and family, Giver of the Good Death and an Angel of God, *la Santisima Muerte* is first and foremost a Saint- a Holy Being- an emissary of God that will usher us to the next world. She is Godmother to all, a source of inspiration and an embodiment of *Memento Mori.* She is used by the outcast as well as the devout, although Her veneration is not sanctioned by the official Church. In the popular media, she is often linked to the *narcotraficantes-* drug traffickers. Her cult in myriad expressions has grown tremendously in popularity, especially in the past two decades. Through all these myriad expressions of Death, there are landmarks and specificities that give both broad palate and specific flavor.

But what of green growing things? And of Death's relationship to them? Perhaps it is as simple as cataloging varied materia magica and medica allied to the Bony Lady. Do not fear! There *will* be plants. And *la Muerte* (who is *always* here). But perhaps there is *more,* I hope. Beyond new lists and new ingredients, I hope there might be something else taking root. I hope for something more landscape and less portrait. There is also a certain familiarity needed, dear reader: *¿podría tutearle?* For we must be able to speak of Death, both yours and mine, without the distant abstractions common to exotification and romanticization, absent formality but never respect. I suspect in the starting of such an article I first must predicate my own understanding of *la Santisima Muerte,* as one not only specific to my explorations and background, but a continued study and fascination complicated by a holistic journey *with* and *to* Her.

My understanding of the Skinny Lady is informed by several factors that are relevant: my specific cultural upbringing as a child of a SoCal Chicana (*somos pochos, ¿y que?*); familial practice; interviews with *muertistas,* candle store owners, and *curanderos* over the last two decades; any textual documentation of Her cult and its practice I could find in English or Spanish both in print and online; and all filtered through my own biases, both known and unknown. I maintain that the Saint is both specific and universal- for Death comes to us all. Let us be clear, here she is born of a Mexican understanding of such, embracing all the hybridity, the myth and reality of the *mestizaje-* the great mixing of cultures that gives rise to *la raza.*

My personal dressing of the Saint as I understand Her is most heavily informed by the wonderfully prismatic practices of Mexican curanderismo, placing *la Muerte* within a cultural contextualization which embraces Death as integral to and inseparable from, Life. She is ever present as part of our experience of this world rather than simply 'on call' as another in the long list of dial-a-saint miracle workers as is commonly reflected in most relations of Her cult and power. I am equally interested in the greater miracles of Purpose and Peace as in the small miracles of every day need.

Through this, my study of the herbal lore of *la Parca* will include some plants that have less to do with Death itself, and more with understanding the Saint as she walks on the soil of multiple inheritances that is Mexico. There are few Saints as universal and equally personal. My Death will be unlike any others, for it is mine to experience; but I too will meet Her in the end. Also, we look at the culture that births this face of Death, to see how She might be understood and engaged, that such a study enriches not only our understanding of *Santisima Muerte,* Holy Death, but our enjoyment of this most holy Life we each are given.

As her cult was bound to familial home altars until the great public coming out of Doña Enriqueta Romero's shrine to Santa Muerte in Tepito, Mexico City, in 2000 (and the subsequent internet dissemination of Her cult) we must immediately battle any projection of dogmatic canon, that great Western tendency perhaps inherited from Abrahamic claims to singular 'correct' belief. Some find *la Muerte* to be very Catholic, others very pagan; some work with Her in many colors, others in three robes, or one; some feel her as an Angel, others as demon; and through all this, we must be aware that the nature of the cult is an expression of Mexico and its people- hybrid, syncretic, multifaceted, complex, and practical.

So we must consider how to walk you, dear one, through this Garden of Death, where do we begin? Of course, as with all things, with tortillas; and after we are properly *satisfecho* on that diet of our ancestors, we move on to bribes, manipulations, and sanctification through a handful of plants both Old World and New. By the end of our time together, I have the hope that the robe in which we each dress our Death may be newly verdant, vivified by that greening power that allows us, like each plant we will explore, to be a part of the cycles of the universe rather than imagine ourselves apart. That each may be a flower, and a song, that poetry may bloom and with it, understanding. What grows, will be cut, but always to be sown again.

Our Lady of Tortillas

While Christianity maintains that humans are born from clay, the Indigenous peoples of Mexico offered that we were made from corn. In Mexica (commonly called *Aztec*) cosmology, the great mother *Cihuacoatl*, Snake Woman, grinds the bones of the previous generation to make the bones of the next, just as we dry and grind corn to make tortillas. So we must begin here, in this cultural examination of that divine plant- *Zea mays* - and its role in understanding our place in the cosmos, our understanding of Life-Death.

I am not proposing a direct link to Mexica cultus nor proposing a solely European origin for the practices of *Santa Muerte*. For years many have debated this, and I find the discussions and arguments around this indicative of how both Mexico perceives itself as well as how Mexico is perceived by the outside world, eternally battling the effects of colonialism, of using the *mestizaje* as both prison and liberator, reason and excuse. I would rather invoke daily practice and inspiration- for while no contiguous link to any Mexica cult has been proven for the origin of *Santa Muerte,* the fact that many who venerate her continue to find inspiration in this proposed origin, while still using the trappings of Roman Catholicism, and embracing the wonderfully complex and beautiful creolized worldview that allows for these multiple inheritances to coexist. *This* is what interests me.

Why is our *Flakita* so popular? Because She answers the needs of a people, because a skeleton can be dressed however it needs to be by those working with Her. So rather than unpack the complex history here in this paper, let me return to invoking pragmatism, of the use of Mexica cosmology as a great unifier and lingua franca since the cultural revolutions of the 20th century because of hundreds of years of detribalization and denial of indigeneity as *part of* the complex tapestry in which we shroud *la Muerte.* A full examination must include everything, including the complex cults of Death and Passiontide from a colonial Iberian Catholic cultural dominance, syncretism with various New Age ideologies and the inheritance of Theosophical and now Neo-Pagan modalities, conflation with and practical exchange with Afro-Caribbean practices like *Santería* and *Palo,* to the influence of commercial spirituality and the *yerbería/botanica* mindset (more products to sell!). All of this bundled in the inheritance of the cultivation of Latin America as a colonial slave state prized for its *use to others*. So in the day to day, where do we find ourselves but in a culture that is at war with its own ancestry, but so clearly a product of such. It is a diet that causes cultural *empacho*, served in little bite sized morsels we can almost digest. So tear off a piece of tortilla and let's start chewing. The cultural context with which we find our Saint should be explored slowly rather than quickly argued over. Culture is something you grow up in, like a bacteria! not a neat list. So, bit by bit. We'll try to drink some *yerba buena* tea after to help with the digestion.

How beautiful is Cihuacoatl! How beautiful is Our Lady of Tortillas! Corn which is grown from ancient seed, which is exposed to the Sun, which is cut and dried, consumed or saved for the future. Here, in this process, it is our bones. And this process is both specific and broad.

It is in the memory of the Divine Feminine Earth, this Serpent Mother who births us and consumes us, where we plant any expression of Mexican spirituality. It is here in these furrows that the cult of Tepeyac–Our Lady of Guadalupe–matures. It is here that *la Malinche* and *la raza* take root. It is here la *Santa Muerte* walks through the corn rows, ready to reap. For the Feathered Serpent gathered the ancient bones of those who had died from the previous creations, and brought them to Serpent Woman. It is Feathered Serpent that added his blood to the *masa* she made from those bones. From this dough, the first man and woman of our Age were shaped, and Feathered Serpent breathed life into them. From this Serpent Energy we are born, we who shed our skins like all beings of the earth. We who like corn shed our husks like all beings of the earth. We who like corn are dried and planted in the earth to be born again. *We who are like corn.*

Humans are tricky to pin down. We like to separate ourselves from nature in many modalities, being the seal of progress rather than a piece of it. So many ways to describe the things that make us what we are, each description often seeking sole claim to authenticity. Tear off more tortilla, friends. We have more to digest!

In our *lingua franca* of contemporary Mexica cosmology, that great umbrella many with detribalized indigenous heritage engage with to understand the universe our ancestors interacted with, there are a number of animistic centers that give life to the world- a number of 'souls'. Humans experience three of these, plants two. Let us begin with commonality then. There is the life force itself, expressed in the *ihiyotl,* the liver soul, which belongs to the world and is inhaled at birth and exhaled at death. This is the soul all in the world has in common that is alive. If it has life, it has *ihiyotl.* It is the 'smelly' life force that allows us to manipulate our essence, but without specific ownership. It is, rather, a shifting, or shaping. It is not individual. It is a separated part of the whole. The *ihiyotl* of plants binds them to their species and environments, and in death, especially in prized exemplars, the *ihiyotl* can hang over the earth in a thick, viscous essence that can bring illness when we are exposed to it before it neutralizes again. It is one the contributors to *mal de aire,* the illness of "bad air", this rot of the life force that can even stalk us or be directed to do so, its memory seeking a container to be *breathed*.

In addition to *ihiyotl,* a plant breaks the surface of the earth to be exposed to the Sun. This act, this exposure to the Sun on a specific day, also brings *tonalli,* the head soul, the soul of time and place, of destiny and potential as expressed in the sacred calendar, as expressed in this comparative astrology. *Tonalli* is unique to each day, the quality of the Sun as it first shines down upon each new life. As fire is brought to the head, for life is hot and death is cold, the quality of this fire is contextualized through an understanding of this *head soul,* which has a quality of individuality even if it is shared by all who come to light on that same day. It is the *tonalli* that can be harvested and seized, giving spiritual strength and succor, it is the *tonalli* that as humans, we share in the quality of the day we were first seen by the Sun.

The calendar round that describes these qualities is also a source of names, for calendar names were the norm until your face was formed, i.e., a personality was clear and could be named in later years. This *tonalli* is borrowed from the Sun, it is not ours, and will return to the heavens upon our death. As heat diminishes in the body, the *tonalli* goes. Interestingly, overexposure to the Sun, the source of *totona*–heat–also kills the body, whether plant or animal. All things in balance, for creation is tricky, and the earth is slippery. We are the children of Serpents, after all. Plants, animals, humans, rituals, buildings, anything bound to time and place and that has a singular moment of exposure to the Sun has *tonalli*.

Now, humans also have *teyolia*–the heart soul– a personality and individuality that extends itself into the world past its own container. We exert extreme influence. The *teyolia* is our passion, our likes and dislikes, and it is the soul that is uniquely ours. It is this soul that flies back to visit relatives on *el Dia de los Muertos*. It is this soul that makes grandma who she is, for it is informed by the *ihiyotl* and wonderfully intertwined with the *tonalli* as it is expressing the role and impact of these two other 'souls' on the body. When we offer our 'heart' we are offering these things that makes us '*us*'.

Each soul can be harvested by *la Parca,* and each soul indeed finds resonance in different expressions and manifestations of, even ways of interacting with, *Santisima Muerte*. Cycles. Of creation. Of generation and generations. The sacrifice of the gods brings movement, life and beginningless, which leads to the sacrifice of humans (both in ritual form and as bodily decomposition), which allows Death as darkness, stillness, and end-ness, to be acted upon to regenerate into life and the cycle continues. Birth and death, grind us down again to raise us up again. *Meet the new boss, same as the old boss.* But bit by bit, friends. There are always more tacos. So, back to the tortilla, we who are like corn.

I invoke corn, but past the specifics of its history and botany, we could be discussing any staple grain. Grains which provide almost half of our caloric intake on average as humans. Grains which become metaphor for life-death and incarnation-resurrection in many religions and beliefs- from the transubstantiation of the host in Catholicism to John Barleycorn to other agricultural deities like Osiris or Dionysus to Attis and others. Corn is a highly cultivated and designed food staple, reared in ancient Mexico and spreading out to become a revered food of two continents. It is also currently a victim of strange machinations that regulations cannot contain as laws do not stop the wind from carrying GMO corn to fertilize non-GMO corn and post-NAFTA exportation of high fructose corn syrup into Mexico contributes to one of the highest obesity rates in the world. Corn is savior and destroyer, for like all things in this lineage of thought, everything contains its opposite, this is what holds the world together.

This duality was not always perceived as oppositional. We interpret it as such now as inheritance of western conceptions of dualism. Indigenous Mexica cosmology expressed pairings of 'opposites' as single concepts: life-death, hot-cold, day-night. It is a subtle shift, but the understanding of spectrum brings process and change as part of the identity rather than destroyers of it. Death, in this way, becomes Life. Here we find a twinning, often referred to as a *cuate*- meaning 'twin', from the nahuatl *coatl*–snake. It is the relationship between the serpent and its shed. Result of the other, a different skin of the same essence. The Virgin of Guadalupe as Life is the *cuate* of Santisima Muerte. They are sisters sharing in the same essence. This is not a Spanish conception. This is a Mexican conception born of that same hybridity as our blood.

Proudly creole. With new *pochismos* to offend and change things, for it is all a process. *Amor y muerte, nada más fuerte.* We are all walking in the Underworld- for this world is the first layer of both Heaven and Hell. We are marching toward the inevitability of Death. To be ground down. We who are like corn. *One does not live forever on this earth: We endure only for an instant!*

Tilling the Garden

Ah, so what grows in the Garden of Death? What makes a plant 'of Death'? Is it the ability to invoke Death? To bring her close? To understand her better? To be able to placate her? To avoid Her? We must walk between our neatly planted rows of phytochemistry and medical botany, and allow the undergrowth of myth and culture to inform us beyond materialism, but not in ignorance of the material.

What is buried is like the Dead. What echoes the process of grain, of incarnation itself, is by nature *holy.* Germination, sprouting, growth, flowering, fruition, dissemination, withering, and decay. Where is our lesson here? Surely, almost all use of plants is necromantic, for the plant is severed from life, where we become Reaper ourselves. If we are wise, we become Creator by recombining such matter into new possibilities, for while the existential life is over, the magical life is immortal. We may gather according to chemistry, by mythic association, by appearance, by location, time or place or any combination of these.

We can look at the anatomy of the plant as sympathetic to *Santa Muerte,* as sharing in her nature or perhaps, nature's. The roots being subterranean invoke the chthonic, the *inframundo* of which She is the Psychopomp Queen. The seed, now rooted, breaks the surface of the soil to expose itself to the Sun, the stem reaching towards the Sun that instills new life. Born of the cold darkness, but tropistically calling to the warmth of the Sun for Life, we open our hands to the blessings of the world, like leaves gathering sunlight.

It must be more than death-bringing plants that call her. For the Death invoked in Santisima Muerte is Holy and Good. She is a force beloved of God, and helps us make the most of our lives. So the 'plants' of Death cannot just be those that bring Death. As Death is in a context here. We shroud our lives in so many variations to give them purpose and meaning, why should our Death be any different? Of course there are affinities for certain plants! But here, too, *mi socio*, let us consider how we navigate the Shrine, how we envision our relationship to both Life and Death, what cultural conceptions and mythic identities both inherited and innovated might there be?

There must be a consideration for funereal herbs, those plants associated with either masking the strong smells of death and decay. We could naturally discuss those plants that echo the smells, but also those plants that make death more palpable are of import. In these small mixtures, we learn to confront the inevitability of *la Sebastiana's* arrows. To inoculate ourselves against the shock of death. To invite her to the table to talk and share and be one with the family. The *abuelita* who asks you your dreams and wants you to achieve them so you can know joy and love in this life. But we each color our lives in different hopes, and so we similarly color our Deaths.

We use plants and offerings to manipulate the medicine to our favor and to the favor of clients. It is a balance of understanding hot and cold- so much a part of indigenous world view, and layering additional humoral understandings inherited from Europe- wet and dry. The balance and manipulation of these qualities brings different results. It changes the *pahtli*, the medicine.

We should consider the impact of Catholicism upon this herbal lore of Death- the cultic expressions and folklore of Passiontide and Calvary and the Harrowing of Hell. Of the herbal lore associated with Good Friday, the day Death took the Son of God into her domain, consuming Jesus in her own form of Communion! And her ultimate role is solidified in this hybrid expression- for she exists to bring value to Life, and take her *cuates* son, as the *comadre* of Jesus, into her embrace. We will die, and there is value in confronting this, embracing it, and as *muertistas* might propose, in loving it. Loving *her*.

Let us also pound the *amatl,* forming the bark into *amate* paper. This is the ancient paper of Mexico, originally made from the guacimilla (*Trema micrantha)* and now also from higuerón (*Ficus tecolutensis*). It forms the codices that document indigenous knowledge. They reflect the very fabric of creation, for the stories start and then unfold accordion-like, allowing one continuous story, with many sections. Violent pounding of the bark makes ideas and images and words flow, giving new life to the husk of something that used to live. And now it lives again.

These are the fibers of everyday existence, the echoes of the past that color our future, the echoes of the future that create our past. For even the Catholic calendar is cyclical, and every Good Friday *la Flaca* will take Jesus, and every year, life will begin again. It is *our* story written every year, allowing us to enter into these Mysteries, knowing both sides of the paper. Knowing how the story ends. You plant a garden to harvest it, after all, no?

Bribery, Essential Nature and Righteous Manipulation

While corn and those mysteries bring fuller understanding, there are also many means to *work* the Saint to our advantage. The time-honored practice of magical bribery enters, the artful manipulation of request and reward that governs the commerce of the Saint. We can look at the food offerings and 'daily maintenance' of her Shrines, where coffee, tobacco, and alcohol and clean water may be given daily to stir the shrine after sleep. Tequila is enjoyment and levity, coffee is alertness and attentiveness, but also a separator from the death-like unconsciousness of sleep, bringing breath and life to the shrine of Death.

We must ask ourselves what is the purpose of these offerings? Purists will say that all she requires is prayer, flowers, candles, and incense, echoing Catholic saints and more orthodox vocabulary of those cults. But this is not echoed in common practice, where fruits and cooked offerings range from simple tortillas and *buñuelos* to cakes to baked fruits and various fruit *atoles* and *champurrados* and fresh *moles.* There is always coffee. *Santa Muerte* has a sweet tooth, and variety is the spice of life!

What do these offerings do? Are they simply an outpouring of thanksgiving? Are they symbols? Are they bribery for miracles to be performed, both large and small? Are they part of the 'energy' required for a successful working? Each *muertista* will have a different answer. For some, it is very much a transaction-based offering system; for others it is a way to show honor and increase the relationship with Her.

We should always remember pragmatism over symbolism in this, and while the symbols sets vary from person to person, there is also an awareness of a certain way of looking at things as qualities of a magical life and an autonomy of each offering as related to its nature and being-ness, rather than as symbol and representation. Why is there water on her shrine? *Because it's wet.* We can't have her bones drying out. "Yes, and" if you will. We color the offerings the way we color her Robes. Different manifestations of how Death walks- in bone, blood, and decay; in longevity, passion, or vitality– here we might start to understand a reflexivity, for what you sow, you reap. Certainly here in the Garden of

Death, it is no different.

A Lottery, and A Mixed Bouquet

> *La muerte tilica y flaca.* [Death, thin and lanky]
> *-Refrán for #14 Lotería Card, la Muerte*

In the popular Mexican *lotería,* often known as "Mexican bingo," there are 54 cards with pictographs, each an archetype (some perhaps, stereotypes), that can be called by the *cantor* as each player checks their *tabla,* their allotted grid of possibilities, then placing rocks or beans or bottle caps on each image that matches what has been called out. There are *refranes* "verses" assigned to each card, allowing a poetic exploration, often in riddle form or pun-like in nature, of each image. Some are based on homophonic puns; others are more philosophical. Others are quite straightforward.

Here let me shout, *¡lotería!* For our survey must by nature be shorter than curiosity and devotion might desire, but in building upon what we have learned, dear reader. The *viriditas* saturated slippery earth of Life-Death as exemplified by corn, in the day souls animated by the Sun, in the life force that stalks at night, we might stir alliances old and new in these few plants. It is this mixed bouquet that death might throw like the bride of Life she is, and each will inform the other, and hopefully help our own *flower-songs* of understanding.

La Muerte walks amongst the *lotería* in card #14. While it is not outright an association with *Santa Muerte,* allow me, friend, to place far more significance on this number than is necessary! Fourteen are the visible finger bones of the hand, fourteen bones wrapped around fourteen plants, to reveal the nature of the fourteenth card as understood by those who straddle two worlds as one people. We must start somewhere to get somewhere, and fourteen at least I can justify with glee and kitsch loyalty, and so our bouquet grows...

Are we to catch the bouquet Death throws?

In looking at the following plants, the main objective is not to provide a complete summary of the plant through history, medical botany and cross-cultural folklore- but rather a context in larger Mexican folklore and its specific relevance to *la Muerte* within various expressions of her worship and workings.

Plumeria | Plumeria spp.

Cacalo-xochitl - "Crow Flower"- this is the flower of ultimate respect. Although in Mayan association it is associated with fertility deities and female sexuality, in Mexica herbal lore it is the flower of nobility and honor. To appear before a person of higher rank than you, to hold a plumeria blossom in your hand allowed your face (symbolic of your personality) to be pleasing. Gardens of plumeria were planted by the houses of nobility. With la Muerte, to bring the crow flower of respect to her, it intensifies the appeal and the weight of your prayers. To leave them with her speaks of her angelic status, a Queen amongst all, the Great Leveler. To understand her role in your own life, as your personal death, that which will take your life, to crown your Death in plumeria allows you to bring respect and honor to your time in this world, calls you to make the most of your mortal life. If you are speaking to her daily, if you have this practice of interacting with her past the occasional ask or need, but rather are exploring her impact in your life beyond 'bought' miracles. To pray, do not just hold in front of your face to acknowledge her nobility, but consider holding it equidistant between her *calaca* and your own. Then you may breathe of each other's divine status, and you may be heard and hear in turn. A treatise could be written on the wonders and mysteries of this plant.

The flower tricks its pollinators by its fragrant night scent, it is a nectarless flower. Still the sphinx months go from flower to flower in vain hoping for the scent-promised nectar. It is easily propagated from stem-tips in Spring, allowing the cuttings to dry at the base before planting in well-draining soil. Cross pollination and grafted cuttings have made many cultivars. As its scent is strongest at night and carried on the wind, it invokes *Yohualli Ehecatl*- the Night Wind- the aspects of the Divine that are invisible and yet easily sensed, moving among us intangibly but potently. Mysterious, but not secret. Native to the New World, its export into other cultures often carried funereal connotations; considered the dwelling place of ghosts and demons, and often planted in burial grounds. Combined with sandalwood, many will recognize its scent as *nag champa* incense. Its aroma invokes with it other strong-smelling flowers relevant to *la Santa*:

- Gardenia (*Gardenia spp.*) - is also said to bring peace and calm to the shrine, and is the flower of the *Catrín* and *Catrína*, the dandy's boutonnière.
- Night blooming cereus (*Epiphyllum oxypetalum*, and also *Selenicereus grandiflorus*), those glorious cacti blossoms whose mandala-like flowers only open once a year, have come to be associated with the preciousness of life, and when in bloom are said to be the Ear of God. Their scent carries for miles when in bloom, and is felt by some workers to speak of the angelic and divine nature of *Santa Muerte*.
- Night blooming jasmine (*Cestrum nocturnum*), called Queen of the Night in Spanish, said to echo the prayers said for the dead and hold them in the

ears of the Virgin Mary to help progress their souls from Purgatory to Heaven, associated with the sanctity of prayer.

- Tuberose (*Polianthes tuberosa*), called *omixochitl*– 'Bone Flower'– by the Mexica, and associated with the anointing of Jesus by Mary Magdalene (invoking Old World spikenard), and is said to bring honor and dignity to those dying, and to speak of devotion both in adorning shrines and through its invocation of the beloved and faithful dead.

The strong alcohol floral washes of ylang ylang (*Cananga odorata*) are said to vibrate similarly, as the liquid Smarties® smell of Siete Machos cologne elicits similar work of these white flowers, bringing protection, dispelling evil spirits, and improving the qualities of the shrine or person that wears it.

Copal | *Bursera glabrifolia* and *B. bipinnata; Protium copal; Copaifera officinalis;* various others

Copalli- nahuatl for "incense"- is the hardened resin of any number of trees used as incense. B. Glabrifolia is considered *macho* (male), while *B. pinnata* is considered *hembra* (female). This is the life blood of a tree, tapped and harvested to elevate the prayers of the devout, to petition the gods and honor the dead, to bring health to the body and to repel pests. It was used as a substitute for frankincense and valued as a cleansing, purifying scent. Referred to poetically as 'the white lady' or 'the white haired lady' (referring to the smoke) it was considered proof of the connection between the worlds. Burned in offering to the many directions, it sanctifies a space and its smell is the very smell of Mexican prayer life.

Copal, the 'prince of incense' is used to describe many

New World resins, and now a few Old World ones as well. It is used in combination with other herbs or resins for suffumigating a space, and to accompany prayer, like musicians accompanying the *flower-songs* of prayer. It is used as a fixative in various crafts and as an adhesive for ritual paper garments and crowns fitted for *la Flaca.* Ancient stories of women who turned into trees, whose blood was collected as copal to communicate with the worlds above and below, are found in many Mexican cultures. It also is used to offer blood in that most controversial of practices- *auto-sacrifice.* Ritual bloodletting is an ancient practice for the pre-conquest indigenous of Mexico. Blood was offered to the gods and dead alike. Royal families often were required to publicly bleed for their people to the point of near death which induced visions. Average people were called upon to offer blood several times a day to help repay the sacrifice of the Gods to make this Age, the Sun, and our own ancestors.

There is great debate about the efficacy and safety of ritual bloodletting, but the historical precedent as a staple of pre-conquest Mexican indigenous religious life cannot be ignored. While ancient methods involved injuring the body with stingray spines or agave needles or special ropes passed through open wounds and the blood caught on amatl paper and then burned, those modern practitioners that continue this practice might favor more sanitary methods, like a dedicated sterilized needle or lancet (like those used for checking blood sugar). Prayers are said, like the *Credo* and a *Padre Nuestro,* and in emulation of the wounds of Jesus, a small drop of blood is smeared onto a single copal grain and then burned. The blood covered copal is said to call the ancestors to witness, stir the attention of God and all the deities, and to personalize the prayer with the thanksgiving of the jade-water of tree and human, drawing comparisons to the nourishing nectar that flows through the flower of our bodies.

Few practices seem to raise as much suspicion and

controversy as auto-sacrifice amongst magical practitioners who ethically view the practice as naïve, karmically dangerous, potentiating lesser spirits, or promoting a miasmic ritual environment. Emically, from the practitioners who embrace the practice, it is sacred, empowering, ancestrally founded, and reverential. Regardless it should not be engaged casually or hastily, but after deep consideration of your own feelings, any ritual elders you may be learning from, and with sanitary precautions undertaken. It is a possibility, or an echo of one. The white haired Lady is a messenger who might be an ally in this manner, or she may remain 'unstained'. White copals are often used for *la Blanca,* the White Robe. Gold copal and mixtures with spices are often used for *la Roja.* Black copals mixed with other ingredients or on its own resonates with *la Negra.* The use of these various copals naturally invokes other resins:

- Frankincense (*Boswellia spp.*), most similar to white copal, it brightens a space and elevates prayer, often felt to be solar and contains anti-depressant properties. Used for all robes, but especially *la Blanca.*
- Myrrh (*Commiphora spp.*), considered funereal/necromantic and 'darker' it brings an added earthiness; a witness to the Divine on Earth, it is the female to Frankincense's male. Along with Frankincense, it is one of the gifts of the *Reyes Magos* to the infant Jesus. Often used with *la Negra.*
- Benzoin (*Styrax spp.*), it is a sweet resin to mix with plant materia without dominating the scent; neutralizing toxins and restoring equilibrium of the shrine and home.
- Dragon's Blood (*Dracaena draco,* among others),

largely used for healing and commanding restless spirits, exorcism and restoring vitality, used in love work with *la Roja* and in exorcism work with *la Negra.*

Tabaco / *Nicotiana genus,* especially *Nicotiana tabacum*

Oh tobacco, you martial wonder plant! This notorious member of the Solanaceae/nightshade family is both celebrated and maligned and has a complex history and similarly multifaceted folklore surrounding it. Some ancient cultivation sites in Mexico date to the first millennium, and its popularity spread through the Americas.

Smoked both socially and ceremonially, it is a major cash crop whose cultivation is well known. So where do we find its connection to *la Muerte*? It starts in the breath, the fouling of the mouth to share in the strong stenches akin to Death. It brings the *cabrona* to the party. For She is a Lady but a Commoner all the same, for who is more regal and more ubiquitous than Death? Cigarettes and cigars are now one of the most common offerings. Blowing smoke upon the *ídolos* both cleanses and strengthens them. Shot-gunning the cigar is considered respectful, for you are not pointing the lit end at Her, and the smoke billows out, cloaking *la Dama* in a temporary robe of smoke.

Tobacco is sacred to *Santa Muerte* in all her manifestations, although many feel cigarettes are more appropriate for some robes than cigars. Similarly, the use of tobacco calls to the use of mota "marijuana" especially considered resonant with *la Blanca,* the White Robe. Those who see a *plática* - a heart to heart- with *la Muerte,* can light up a cigar and offer *un cafecito* or a shot of tequila and pray a *Padre Nuestro* and three *Ave Marias* while smoking, paying attention to how the lit end burns, and watching how the ashes fall onto a plate. Read in various manners, the cigar becomes offering, revitalizer, and divinatory aide.

Datura | Datura spp.

Devil's Trumpets, Witch Tree, Mother of Madness, Thorn Apple, called *Toloache* from Tolohuaxihuitl in nahuatl "the plant with the nodding head" in reference to the *datura spp.* seed pods, these infamous nine members of the Solanaceae family, are perpetually associated with witchcraft, night flight, shape shifting and maleficia. Shrubs with evening blooming trumpet shaped flowers produce a seed pod (with or without thorns based on specific species), that easily identifies the plant at a distance. The peppery smell of the leaves and sweet smell of the flower are also easily remembered. The root can be dug and shaped, similar in lore to the European mandrakes, and the ritual preparations of it are so variable that no 'safe' recommendation can be made. Even experts in working with *Mama Verde* and her medicine will not guarantee safety or propose a 'correct' dosage. While I am all for *psychonautic* exploration, some medicines are best avoided than recommended without more personalized mentorship.

A strong ally to the *nahuales,* the shapeshifters and skin-walkers, and the witches that fly through the air accompanied by the *alibrijes,* fantastical spirit animals, or even fly as various birds themselves are aided by this plant. Seven of the nine species of datura are native to Mexico, and her place as bringer of magic and madness is such that to speak of her at all is to open oneself up to a lifelong study. She is used in love and fertility magic with *la Roja,* and is said to be a mother to countless restless spirits in the roadside ditches and foothills of the mountains. Her dried fruits are often found on altars for *la Negra* and other sorcerous inclined robes of *la Santa.* They can be filled with other ingredients in powdered form and used in spiritual warfare, or used to cover another working you wish to remain unseen.

In the wake of datura, we must consider that quintessential Witch Tree, the Angel Trumpet- *Brugmansia* in all her manifestations, for the lore of the tree daturas is so universal in Latin America that it is synonymous with witchcraft. To become a witch, it is said you merely need sleep under a tree in bloom. Her pendulous blossoms are prized soaked in wine to add her similarly toxic medicine to be celebrated, with precaution. It is the axis mundi of hell, fed by the underground river the witches use to navigate out of the Dream world and Hell both. Similarly, we bring the *teonanácatl* to witness, those "little teachers" of Maria Sabina and the "flesh of the gods" that are *Psilocybe* mushrooms. The hallucinogenic effects of *psilocibina* are considered preferred to the daturas' rather toxic inconsistency. Those beautiful bindweeds *(Convolvulus)* and morning glories (*Ipomoea*) whose seeds contain psychoactive ergoline alkaloids are kin to our celebrated daturas, with their own complex folklore and use by the witches of ancient and modern Mexico.

Muicle | Justicia spicigera

The beautiful Mexican honeysuckle is a small evergreen shrub with bright orange tubular flowers that grows throughout Central America. Its color attracts butterflies and hummingbirds, which in Mexican thought are the souls of Warriors who have died in battle, connected to the vitality of the Sun and symbolic of life and protection. But the hidden secret of Muicle is not just in its beauty or pollinator prowess, when you boil its leaves, the water turns deep indigo blue. This blue is said to avert the evil eye, reflect malevolent spirits, and bring peace. It renews vows and restores grace, just as it makes white whiter by its use as a laundry bluing! To revitalize the Robe of la Blanca, rinse the white cloth with leaves of Muicle. To hide the White Robe from the workings we sometimes appeal to *la Negra* for, veil her in muicle rinsed cloth to keep her refreshed. The leaf-water can be used to sprinkle over her freshly cleaned altar to restore the 'spiritual light' the shrine emanates. Similarly, the Black Robe can be draped in a simple *rebozo* dyed with oak gall and walnut shells, with Muicle added to bring a less harsh resonance, and to enrich the color, if not to provide variance to the various fibers used to weave the cloth used as robe. Similarly, one can wash the hands with the blued water mixed with holy water after a funeral or after touching the Dead, to cleanse and restore vitality.

Maguey / *Agave spp.*

Mother of Inebriation, Mother Who Clothes Us, Mother who makes us bleed! *Mayahuel,* the Mexica *teotl* of the Maguey, is a maternal and fertility goddess. Her fibers can be used to make rope and even cloth. Her thorns can be used to draw blood in ritual sacrifice. Her sap can bring inspiration or inebriation. Maguey is the source of the fermented heart sap known as *octli,* or *pulque,* that milk colored sour yeasty divine drink of the gods, and discovered by Opossum, who became the first drunk. O Pulque, liquid courage! Liquid inspiration! *But must it smell like stale semen?* For the Mexica, inebriation was a divine state, but not necessarily a desired one, one reserved for elderly people who had served society, and as a ritual intoxicant. Losing your utility and agency was never desirable for the young and capable, indeed it is echoed in that very loaded insult 'inútil". Our plant, maguey, is anything but useless! Do not let the *Centzon Totochtin* "the Four Hundred Rabbits" seduce you with their rampant excess!

The cloth made from the fibers is easily turned to rope, or when mixed with other fibers, like cotton (another thorned textile plant!), makes a good cloth. The *tilma* of Juan Diego that is now enshrined in the Cathedral at Tepeyac is emblazoned with the image of *la Guadalupana*. The Virgin is on maguey cloth. *But does she drink pulque?!* Certainly *Santa Muerte* does, and the distilled versions, *mescal* and *tequila*. Colors are the easy part, silver for *la Blanca*, añejo for *la Roja*, and pulque for *la Negra*. Yet, there is so much more to our plant.

The plant is also associated with its own specific Virgin Mary, known as *la Virgen de los Remedios*, the Virgin of the Remedies, who appeared in an agave plant the night before the fall of Tenochtitlán and the Aztec Empire known as the Noche *Triste*, where a statue carried by the Spanish (and known for her aide in the *Reconquista* of Spain), was hidden under a maguey plant and came to life to throw sand in the face of their enemies.

The use of the thorns for bloodletting is of great value, whether engaging in the practice, or in understanding the value of offering such thorns *to Her*. Our life is visited by little deaths constantly. We who are like corn are sensitive to the Sun and its blasting heat. This lack of balance can be harmful, fly too close to the Sun, Icarus, and we know what happens. *Conflagration is so Catholic. Burning hearts and all that.*

These little deaths we are exposed to, they hint at the Spanish replacement for Maguey's vast lore, the humble aloe plant. *Aloe spp.* was brought into Mexico and thrived in the hot climate. Many species are becoming naturalized. Because it is a succulent, it has a fleshy watery gel on the inside of its leaves. This gel has great healing properties, and the serrated, but rarely dangerous leaf edges, echo the American Aloe, another name for Maguey. Many believe the lore surrounding aloe in Mexico is an inheritance of the legacy of Maguey. Aloe assuages the over exposure to the Sun, healing those little deaths. Pulled out of the ground, roots and all, it is often used on small altars and shrines by hanging it upside down and tied to a central point. Hanging upside down to the left of the shrine it is protective from harmful spirits and hanging from the right side of the altar it attracts good spirits. Many hang several different plants around *Santa Muerte's* shrine to bring the blessings and benefits of this plant to their relationship with Her. There is a tradition of aloe rosaries for healing and protection, where a branch of aloe is broken off, and one recites the rosary prayers by using the aloe leaf to mark the prayers, sliding the torn off of the plant off the sheath of the leaf. Even a single decade performed in this manner is felt to enervate and amplify the healing and protective powers of the aloe, and the gel torn off in this way can be used to great effect. Aloe, who is like Maguey, who clothes us, makes us bleed, and drunk.

Cacao / *Theobroma cacao*

Cacao, whose Latin name means 'food of the gods', was one of many treasures discovered by the gods in a mountain storehouse, given to humans after we were first created by Serpent Woman, a gift from our Father Plumed Serpent who bled on the stolen bones of our Ancestors. In tribute to his sacrifice, the cacao pod was decorated in blood won from auto-sacrifice. It was a ritually acceptable substitute for the human heart. The *yollotl* which contained the *teyolia* of the person, passion, personality, identity, that gives us existence. In its natural state, cacao is extremely bitter, its nahuatl name is *cacahuatl,* or bitter water. Valuable enough to be used as currency, it promoted exchange and trade and community. It was considered a powerful intoxicating medicine dangerous to women (no wonder *la Muerte* loves it!).

Chocolate, with its range from naturally bitter to heavily sweetened, or with other complimentary flavors, there is great beauty in this spectrum. As we shroud Death in Robes we understand, cacao can similarly be colored. In offering and practice, the cacao pod and pure dark chocolate is appropriate for all, but very commonly it is put before *la Negra,* milk chocolate or chili pepper or "Mexican" chocolate, which is very sweet and has a strong cinnamon flavor is given to *la Roja,* and white chocolate is given to *la Blanca.* But like all of these tailored offerings, the separation is at once artificial and also ingenious. For each Robe has its origins, its own mythos. Each Robe's nature reflects this mythic construct.

Cacao stirs and wakes up our Death. Life is difficult, and cacao is an understanding of this mystery. When a child was born, the Mexica announced to the child that life was war, and their destiny was battle. This is the thing we must realize, to enjoy life is to actively wrestle with it. Battle does not mean it is unpleasant, and each person's journey is their own. Cacao is a new vantage, even prophecy, and conjures new possibilities, it brings new life and hope. It activates the spirit allies and fortifies the connection to the *tonalli.* It vivifies the shrine, it increases the efficacy of prayers, and magnifies all other offerings. It brings clarity and enjoyment through understanding. In different forms, it sweetens, entices, attracts, and persuades. Make your *champurrado* and your hot chocolate and your *moles,* dear ones. There is much celebrating to do. Chocolate mimics and activates infatuation. Fall in love with life, then! Put your heart on the Shrine of Death! Even in our agony, we can celebrate, for we only live once upon the Earth!

Pericon | *Tagetes lucida*

Texas Tarragon, Mexican Marigold, called *yauhtli* in Nahuatl, is a perennial marigold with anise scented leaves. Its bright orange flowers are said to call to the Dead, especially in the winged forms of butterflies. Orange is associated with the victorious dead, those celebrated heroes who die in battle. It is the sweet herb used to bring blessings into the life of the person who is swept with it in cleansing passes known as *barridas,* often paired ritually with *estafiate* as a bitter counterpart. Much is written of the plant, its associations with rain and fertility, its use in 'sacrificial' powders blown into the faces of the sacrificial victims to 'sweeten' the offering, although they are usually documented as 'stupefying' powders. A similar powder mixed with copal and rosemary brings sweetness back to a shrine after a strong working of protection, and allows the shrine to rest and open again after 'darker' workings. It can be mixed with tobacco to soften the visions and harshness of that ally. It is a flavoring in some *pan de muerto*, and the ancient flower used to open the road from the Cemetery to the House to invite the dead, and ritually it was replaced by the imported pot marigolds we now see on the *ofrendas* for the dead in early November.

Rose / *Rosa spp.*

Finally, the Queen of Flower, that perfect offering, the Rose. In all her manifestations, the rose comes to represent beauty and the precious fragility of life. It is the Virgin standing on the snake (the thorns), the proof demanded of the Juan Diego to validate his vision of *Tonantzin*, the Virgin of Guadalupe, that apparition of the Virgin Mary that appeared to unite the peoples of the Americas, demanding a Temple to her be built as mother of Teotl-Dios (the nahuatl AND Castilian Spanish words for God). It is she who asks *Cuix amo nican nica nimonantzin? No estoy yo aqui que soy tu madre? Am I not here, I who am your mother?* The Rose is the foreign flower accepted on native soil- an offering speaking to the brevity and sanctity of life. It is the miracle of the incarnation of Jesus, and his sacrifice on the Cross, the pains of the Passion and the Crucifixion. This relationship between the beautiful blossom and sharp thorn echoes the non-oppositional dualism to essential to understanding Mexica conceptions of the universe.

While many flowers might adorn her shrine, giving preference to roses, carnations ("spicy" flowers), gladiolus and lilies (and other 'stalked flowers') is not uncommon. While we can color code roses to each Robe, here the tribute to Life-Death is evident. Taking six white roses (or carnations, or any white flower), and placing them in a terracotta pot with three or seven coins, place freshwater and take this to the wall of the Cemetery, or the mouth of a cave, or some place you find resonant with her. This is a tribute, a way of starting to work with her, as commonly practiced Stateside along the Border. Six is a traditional number of Death, but here it is the roses (who many will argue should have the thorns removed. *Ah, Death, where is thy sting?* Speak to me as flowers celebrating the beauty of Life, now being brought to Death. What mysteries are we exploring in this? To give flowers to the Dead, to Death herself? Offering the potential for life, the brevity of beauty, the transience of joy: it is a celebration, a payment, and an invitation. Once we understand that, we celebrate with *Xochiquetzal* and *Xochipilli,* the Feathered Flower and Flower Prince. Our words become celebrated *flower-song* poetry and we engage la Muerte as *Santisima* "the holiest" Muerte. *Nuestra Señora de la Santa Muerte.* Universal but personal. The mystery of the Rose. Like Juan Diego, proof of our contact with the Divine. *No estoy yo aquí que soy tu madre?*

> "It is madness to hate all roses because you got scratched with one thorn. To give up on your dreams because one didn't come true. To lose faith in prayers because one was not answered, to give up on our efforts because one of them failed. To condemn all your friends because one betrayed you, not to believe in love because someone was unfaithful or didn't love you back. To throw away all your chances to be happy because you didn't succeed on the first attempt. I hope

that as you go on your way, you don't give in nor give up!". - *Le Petit Prince,* Antoine de Saint-Exupéry

Adorn her shrine in flowers. Let the sweet scents of flowers fill your home. To engage Life with purpose takes consistent effort. To engage Death with purpose we must practice while living. There are many thorns, but crowning them all is that Flower of Life.

Will flowers be carried to the Kingdom of Death?

The earth is a grave and nothing escapes it,

nothing is so perfect that it does not descend to its tomb.

Rivers, rivulets, fountains and waters flow,

but never return to their joyful beginnings!

-Nezahualcoyotl , 15th Century King of the City State of Texcoco (Pre-Conquest Mexico)

There is some beautiful promise in this garden path; a resonance between us and the plants who help us serve, honor and understand Santisima Muerte. There is a hint of the belief that some plants are even the remnants of earlier creations from failed ages past. They are the bones of ancestors who were not ground down by *Cihuacoatl.* A memory of where we were, all engaging in the unfolding process of creation that is this current age. For we are in the Sun of Movement, an age of cycles and patterns, of predictability and direction. This permeates the fibers of creation as we know it and we are bound to this cycle of Life-Death, holy in nature, awesome in breadth, in this tension that holds the universe together.

For those who tread on this slippery earth, our experience of death is both devastatingly alone and yet in perfect company. For She will be there, turning around from beyond the reach of our left hand, and we find our *techichi* dog, our *xolotl,* manifesting to guide us as we descend deeper into the soil like roots preparing for winter. As our bodies are stripped of the flesh robes we donned in life, as heat and breath leave the body, as the *tonalli* returns to the sky, as the *ihiyotl* returns to serpent-skirted world, as the *teyolia* tries to remember its life and also, its trajectory. Memory blossoms in our progeny, in the seeds of our planted hopes. Some part of us, perhaps the soul offered by the friars and priests in baptism and watered by the Blood of the Man nailed on the Tree. Perhaps this is eternal, and like the *tonalli* joins a collective grace in the skies above. What happens after, past decay, past the certainty of Death, is for the Dead to answer. She is the key and door, for She takes us into the dark. Into the cold. After the four-year pilgrimage, we turn to meet Her in Her throne room, where she accepts our bones, when the last of our descendants has forgotten our name, forgotten what nectars draw the butterflies of our souls to visit this Living House again. She accepts them, perfect and complete, wrapping them in painted bark paper, saving them for future generations, in this age, or perhaps, the next.

For we are the children of multiple inheritances; we are each like a seed planted in foreign soil. Planted in the ground, we become food for our own descendants, and nourish the growth of the world in our decay. Perhaps it is such that plants are the masters, farming us in a fashion, convincing us to grow them and spread their seed that we may die in time to feed their own growth. A willing engagement and bond. As always, we only think we are in control. Neither Death nor Life is permanent, but this life is just once, a rose unlike any other. We are harvested by *la Niña Blanca* like all things of this world for She stands at the left hand of God.

Dressed in the paper garments of the death gods, of the paper tunics the supplicants of the Crossroads Women, waving painted paper flags of devotion and honor, we find these very pages perhaps adding a new robe to our glorious *Madrina.* These words are one robe of many, made of ink shed on paper, with which to cloak the bare bones of our Death, who stands before us like the Virgin Mary in May, wreathed in this mixed bouquet. It is, after all, an exploration but not a dogmatic definitive. For Death is simple, and we make Her complex. For we are all *pochos,* dear readers, the [overripe] fruit does not fall far from the tree of our cultures, and we change what we receive both with intent and without. Let it be celebrated, this movement of our age. This mutation of memory. We who are like corn. We are the growing of the Earth, the shedding of its skin, a consciousness born of the friction of the universe grinding us to make future use of what could not grow in this lifetime. Our *Santa* Muerte reaps all. How beautiful is Death, how holy is Life! May your Death be divine, may your divinity be present in your Death. May *Santa Muerte* remind us all to live and love! *Bendita la muerte cuando viene después de buen vivir.* Death is blessed when it comes after a good Life.

> *Thus, the old ones said*
> *that who has died has become a god,*
> *they said: 'He has been made a god there,' or 'He has died.'*
> -Nezahualcoyotl , 15th Century King of the City State of Texcoco (Pre-Conquest Mexico)

> *Veneramos la muerte, porque la muerte nos da la vida!*
> We venerate death, because death gives us life!
> - Lila Downs

Western Cultural Denial of Plant Sentience and How Shamanic Cultures Interact with Plant Consciousness

Brita Wynn-Dinsmore

Culture has a strong influence on how we perceive the world around us. The term used in anthropology is *enculturation,* which means to learn a first language, culture, and worldview. We then become educated within that cultural worldview. Most of what we think, believe and do while we are young arises, in some form, from the process of enculturation. As we get older and/or travel, and come in contact with other cultures and world views, we may *acculturate,* which is to adopt or learn a secondary culture, which may lead us to question some of what we take for granted as truth in our primary culture. Our Western non-indigenous culture is composed of our core structures of belief about the world, both religious and secular. We are genetically programmed to receive a culture and a language; it is the survival strategy of all the great apes and monkeys. We do not generally inherit behavior[1]. We do not come into this world knowing instinctively what to do or eat to survive but rather, are programmed with culturally flexible learned behavioral strategies for adaptation by the cultural world we see and operate within.

---

[1] American Association of Physical Anthropologists, 1996 (AJPA 101), 569-570.

There are still many kinds of cultural strategies in the world, with very different structures, beliefs, and sciences. The opposite end of the spectrum from an industrialized, state organized culture such as our own would be nomadic foraging culture. All traditional foraging cultures are shamanic, which means the religious specialist that they have is also their healer. Their survival strategies include teaching that plants are contactable, conscious beings with wisdom they will share. Shamans work within many different mediums and realities. They use many techniques to connect with plant and animal consciousnesses as sentient beings (self-aware). They may use hallucinogenic plants to guide them, but they may also use sound and song and sand paintings, dreaming and chanting, vision questing, and trance. What they all have in common is plant relationships that provide valuable wisdom in their interactions with humans, and protocols for healing ourselves and our environment. I have included some examples below from various traditional cultures.

The Luiseno of Southern California, near Mt Palomar and toward the coast are a good example of this approach. This culture used Hallucinogenic plants in male puberty ceremonies. After ritual purification, the Tribal leaders gave the boys Toloache (Datura) to drink. They would then dance until unconscious.[2] This induced colorful and mystical visions and weeks of heightened sensitivity and receptivity. In the glow of heightened sensitivity, "elders imparted songs, dances, and sacred knowledge to the initiates. A sand painting representing the entire cosmos, was made on the ground.[3] Laid out before the initiates was a symbolic universe which included the astronomical and the spiritual, animals, plants,

---

[2] Malcomlm Margolin, *The Way We Lived: California Indian Stories, Songs & Reminiscences, Heydey Books and the California Historical Society* (1993), 24-25.

[3] ibid, 25.

etc. In these shamanic actions, we see a strategy for directly connecting children to the natural world in a deeper way as they transition from childhood to adulthood, that honors and verifies all they experienced in nature in early childhood.

The Bakairi, natives of Brazil believe that "beings" from a sacred realm, inhabited by supernatural beings, live inside animals and plants. They believe these beings can be seen by people, but usually stay hidden. These spirits can be contacted and manipulated by shaman. After a long period of training, they learn to contact and direct specific spirits that they develop special relationships with. These spirits help the shaman cure disease and perform other "magic" such as sorcery against their enemies.[4] The Bakairi use ritual mask dancing, which is related to their cosmography, which is the aspect of culture which deals with intangibles such as ideas and values, to help them distinguish between the sacred and the profane.[5]

The Mardu people of Australia connect to their natural environment and the life within it through ritual and dreaming. The Mardu consider the Dreaming to be the source of all new knowledge, which they believe is transmitted to humans by spirit being intermediaries that bridge the spiritual and human realms.[6] The Mardu see the wholeness in their cosmic order, which includes human society, the plants and animals, and the physical and spiritual environment. This relationship maintains unity that ensures a continuous conduit for the flow of life force power from the spirit world.[7]

---

[4] Debra Picchi, *The Bakairi Indians of Brazil: Politics, Ecology, and Change*, 2nd edition (Long Grove, Illinois: Waveland Press, Inc, 2006), 148.

[5] ibid, 147-148.

[6] Robert Tonkinson, *The Maraud Aborigines: Living the Dream in Australia's Desert*, 2nd edition, (Wadsworth Pub Co, May 1, 2002), 22.

[7] ibid, 22.

The Mardu associate with the spirits who help them in many ways. Some are said to be messengers between spiritual and human realms and are believed to take a continuing interest in human affairs. They are believed to maintain ultimate control over the reproduction of all plants, animals and humans.[8]

So "The Dreaming is a fundamental and complex conception, not only embracing the creative past and the ordering of the world, but having great relevance to the present and the future aboriginal existence."[9] For the Mardu, the Dreamtime still exists, as reality that is happening at the same time as everyday reality and is a vital foundation of the culture. The Dreaming is very important because it is believed to be the source of all power, realized in response to ritual performance. It is viewed as also available to individuals every day in situations of altered consciousness such as dreaming, dance, emotional intensity, and ritual. This allows a brief transcendence of the physical, in which they can tap into the vast reservoir of creation and to consciousness.[10] Children are enculturated that the Dreamtime is in some ways more real than the physical existence and certainly more important than the minutiae of daily existence. They are taught that they can go to this Dreamtime reality like a library and access information and power through connection with the creative forces of nature controlled by the spirits in the Dreaming realm. Further, these spirit relationships are kin based. The spirits themselves are revered as elders, considered ancestral, and are a part of the human family. The Mardu do not pray, prostrate themselves, or sacrifice to communicate with the spiritual realm. They believe that when ritual is properly enacted, the ancestral elders/relatives understand and

---

[8] ibid, 22.

[9] ibid, 21.

[10] ibid, 21.

reciprocate, so are obliged to provide rain, babies, flora, and fauna of which they are also a part.[11]

These cultural worldviews consciously connect with plants and animals daily and interact with nature as a collection of sentient consciousnesses. These world views in contrast are very different from our own cultural structure where the religious specialist is completely separate from the health care professional. We are taught that illness has no energetic component. It is instilled early in Western "enculturative" training that curing illness is just a matter of finding the right chemical or mechanical "therapy," and that diet and plant use has no effect other than as a placebo. Plants only contain chemicals that, if purified in the correct way by a chemist, can become useful drugs. Conventional medicine only arises from treatments verified by the Western scientific method.

As a college professor in the hard sciences and social sciences, I find our cultural ideas about what is considered valid science to be curious and perhaps incomplete and even intolerant of other world views about what is, in fact, observable. Western scientific method states that a hypothesis can only become a theory or law if it can be observed with the senses, in real life experiences by researchers, and that it must be repeatable by others.[12] Though I can tell you, at least in the arena of cultural observation, human behavioral science, and studies not conducted in a laboratory setting, repeatability can be challenging, if not impossible.

Even in that situation, there is the validity of the observation, if the recognized observer is some sort of specialist in the area of study. So, what we can observe through the five senses identified by science hundreds of

---

[11] ibid, 23.

[12] Samantha M. Hens, *Method and Practice in Biological Anthropology: A Workbook and Laboratory Manual for Introductory Courses, Second Edition,* (Pearson Prentice Hall).

years ago (sight, sound, smell, touch and taste,) is the first step in scientific discovery.

But what about cultures who actively use and believe there are other realms and additional senses, such as remote sensing, empathic sense, telepathy, an ability to see the body's energy field, and the "hearing of ghosts and plants." What if these senses are different from person to person like the ones Western culture recognizes? Vision, for example, is variable in lots of ways. Color blindness, distance vision, night vision, and some people can literally see more colors than others. Do all visual observers have the same visual experience? Of course not, but we consider their observations to still be valid unless their visual observation is culturally not accepted as valid.

There is evidence to support that additional senses may exist. Military use of remote sensing abilities is well known, and the police also sometimes use people with remote sensing abilities[13] to find missing persons with enough success that they justify the cost of such use. Other cultures use empaths as healers and medical intuitives with very high success,[14] and then of course, those who see energy fields can be verified by Kirlian photography which can capture photos of the field.[15] Hearing ghosts and plants is an interesting one because there are many documented encounters with ghosts where people say they have heard spirits speak, or have heard the sounds made by them, such as screams, etc.

Interestingly we are more likely to accept these observations as truth because of the use of technology to

---

[13] Paul H. Smith, *Reading the Enemy's Mind: Inside Star Gate: America's Psychic Espionage Program*, (Doherty Associates, LLC, Tom).

[14] Carolyn Fishel Sargent and Thomas Malcolm Johnson, *Medical anthropology: contemporary theory and metho*d (Praeger: University of Michigan, 1990).

[15] Beverly Rubik, "The Human Biofield and a Pilot Study of Qigong," Accessed 26 August 2001.

record such events, than we are to accept that plants may be able to communicate with us. Plants can broadcast scents and sounds that affect animal brains in profound ways,[16] which when using essential oils of said plants, is then called aromatherapy. Is it not likely that those who live in nature can also understand what these scents are communicating? Sadly, studies of such abilities and events are generally labeled pseudoscience by established Western science, are dismissed as imaginary and are pursued no further.

In the Western educational system, if we talk about plants at all to children, we talk about what plants local tribes of Native Americans eat, what plants they should be afraid of, such as marijuana, and what plants are weeds and need to be eliminated from their lawn. Plants are viewed as being unimportant, unnecessary and unconscious, except as natural resources for our use for things like paper towels and toilet paper, and to be pretty and color coordinated in our garden. Children here are taught that plants have no consciousness, that they do not feel, that they do not communicate with each other or with humans, and that they do not actively participate in their surroundings other than to respond to soil and sun and produce oxygen.

What if plants really are capable of conscious sentient communication with humans, and we are enculturating a blindness when it comes to plants, into our culture's children? Consider, for example, the sense of sight. The eyes are lenses for images, and it is the brain that interprets those images and "sees." So, what we see and recognize and even mentally accept as real, is programmed in by culture. The evidence of plant sentience is all around us daily, but are we blind to it because we have been taught that it does not exist?

---

[16] Daniel Chamovitz, "What a plant knows: a field guide to the senses," *Scientific American* (Farrar, Strand & Giroux, 2012).

There are many common experiences that verify plant consciousness and sentience every day. Besides personal accounts from shamans, herbalists, and empaths, there is scientifically collected data on plant consciousness. For example, plants respond favorably to some environments, music, and people more so than others, even when basic needs are met from a scientific perspective such as soil composition, and necessary exposure to sunlight. The variables that are not typically considered are things like music exposure, being talked to and touched in various ways, and "listened" to.

In ethnographic observational studies in shamanic cultures, shamans around the world repeatedly tell researchers that they talk to plants and learn information directly from them[17]. They say that plants tell them what they can do and how to use and prepare them in various ways. The communication comes in visions, in dreams and meditations, and in direct conscious interaction with them in nature including through the use of plants with ego dissolving effects such as Ayahuasca[18] and Peyote. Some Westerners are drawn to these practices and make long journeys into remote locations in hope of connecting to themselves and their relationship with nature deeply.

Shamans are helpful in these cases because they are astute observers in nature and pay attention to every scent, every shape, every interaction observable, because nature is everything to them. It isn't a place they visit once a week; it is their home environment where they live daily life and have multiple interactions with nature throughout each day. They are far more familiar with the natural world than pretty much

---

[17] Kathleen Daley, "Plant Spirit Shamanism: Hearing the Call of the Plants," November 13, 2017, www.pachamamaalliance.org.

[18] Douglas S. Main, "Ayahuasca Can Help You Communicate with Plant Spirits and Heal your Body and Mind," *News Week* (January 25, 2015) https://www.newsweek.com/ayahuasca-can-help-you-communicate-plant-spirits-and-heal-your-body-and-mind-296226.

everyone in Westernized culture. In addition, they are never taught that plants are unconscious things whose value lies only in what humans can use them for.

Foragers (formerly known as hunter/gathers) are taught that all plants and animals are brothers and sisters to humans, that they are equal in sentience and that they are family. "To live in a world in which everything was animate and had personhood was to live in a world of endless potentiality. The most common objects around you were filled with power, intelligence, and even sexual desire, making for a thoroughly unpredictable and magical world."[19]

A shaman is trained to live in a state of 'exstasis,' a term in Greek which means outside the normal states of consciousness. They are masters of altered states of consciousness and awareness in which normal roles of Newtonian three-dimensional existence are no longer valid. Ordinary consciousness is viewed as a kind of sleepwalking. Shamans are viewed as awakened to true reality. To dismiss this as "only imagination" is a gross denial of not only the realm of the possibility, but of any understanding of how the universe really works. Further, imagination is where all things are conceived and can then become reality.[20]

Shamanic healers generally view sickness as loss of power or energy.[21] Even some larger state-organized non-western cultures recognize this concept. One such culture is the Chinese and their recognition of the flow of life force energy (chi) and what can happen when it is blocked or

---

[19] Malcolm Margolin, *The Way We Lived: California Indian Stories, Songs & Reminiscences*, (Heydey Books and the California Historical Society, 1993), 91.

[20] Michael J. Harner, *Way of the Shaman*, 10th anniversary edition, (New York: Harper Row), 40-56.

[21] Sandra Ingerman, "The Power of Shamanism to Heal Emotional and Physical Illness," (2012), http://www.sandraingerman.com/sandrasarticles/abstractonshamanism.html.

impaired in some way.[22] They treat these kinds of ailments with plants that are thought to increase or open the flow of Chi into the body to attain normal energetic balance. In the shamanic cultural worldview, illness is caused by separation from nature, community, source and even oneness. Plants can provide a link back to that connection.

Western culture is also very distrustful of nature, which of course compounds that Western worldview that it is not home, nor friendly. Western stratified religious systems have taught that nature is for our use. They have taught us that nature is soulless, godless, and unconscious. Evangelical world views dismiss natural sentience as well. The Catholic worldview that I was taught and grew up in says that god created everything for our use, not that we are part of a family, and that using nature in ways that are damaging to the ecosystem doesn't matter because 'the last days are coming' and the only thing that really matters is that we have been good Christians and will be 'sitting at the right hand of god.'

Interestingly, my grandmother always talked about trees as conscious beings. She sang to them and sat with them. She would cry when we drove by clear cut forest because she said she could hear them screaming in pain. She was always a major gardener and plants produced for her and bloomed for her with a gloriousness that I've not seen or been able to fully achieve.

She taught me how to transplant with my bare hands so I could feel when and where roots were hanging on to the soil and carefully loosen them without harm. She believed that the spirits people sometimes see in the forest belong to trees. It was confusing to get such mixed messages within the same family and my grandmother was told many times not to fill

---

[22] Acupuncture and Massage College, "What is Qi? Definition of Qi in Chinese Medicine," (August 28, 2017), https://www.amcollege.edu/blog/qi-in-traditional-chinese-medicine.

my head with "fantasies" and "fairy tales." My father's admonishments never stopped her from teaching us to be respectful and loving to plants and trees. My grandmother was not part of any structured belief system, but rather a spiritualism that was passed down for generations on my mother's side of the family.

It took many years for me to sort through the mixed messages, but when I started to formally study herbalism in my early 30s, I found that much of the plant use knowledge learned from my grandmother was consistent with what I was learning. My first herbal program teacher was not terribly science oriented or trained. She talked about herbs as conscious beings with whims and moods. It irritated me at first because at the time I was completing a graduate program in the social and physical sciences and I felt my teacher was lacking in scientific training to be teaching herbal medicine. She was however, a very effective healer, and so I completed the program. It was during that program that I and others in the class started to sense plant consciousness in a way that actually helped heal some pretty serious ailments experienced by some students in the class. One such case was when the spirit of the poke plant came forth with an invitation to please "eat me" to a student who did not yet know that she had a serious lymphatic infection known as mononucleosis. When she received her labs, we identified the plant talking to her as Phytolacca americana. We looked up the plant's known uses in the "American Horticultural Society Encyclopedia of Herbs & Their Uses"[23] for information and it listed a whole host of viral lymphatic infections it can be used for. It then became clear the plant knew what she needed and was trying to help her. We trusted our information and the plant's message and tinctured the berries and she treated the illness with poke for five days. Another set of labs were taken and she was clear for

---

[23] Deni Brown, *Encyclopedia of Herbs and Their Uses*, Dorling Kindersling Books.

the disease in just five days of taking the extract of this plant, with no negative side effects.

After graduation from my academic program, I started teaching and looked for more science-based plant info. It was when I was in an herbal program with an oncologist that I realized that this was part of the journey. It inspired me to dive deeper into studies of ethnobotany, shamanism, and entheogenic use by healers around the world. I started to experience that screaming my grandmother talked about and "hear" more clearly the voices of the plants I grew and worked with. I never talked about these things with any colleagues because of the danger it could pose to my academic career. Educated people tend to label you as crazy and compromised, or "going native," and uneducated people fear you may be dangerous and evil.

This common response stems from the time period broadly described as the "witch craze" or Catholic inquisition. It was taught at that time that nature was the avenue through which Satan could influence humans away from God. Nature is innocent and not sentient or possessing of a soul and therefore is defenseless against evil. Church doctrine actively taught that nature is dangerous, wildness is dangerous, pleasure is dangerous, and of course because of that, the people who heal using nature and plant wisdom, or who enjoy the blissful sensuality of plants, are dangerous. Never forget that organized religion is a social control structure that is used to establish what is good and bad in society for the purpose of maintaining hierarchical power over people.

This doctrine of blindness and mistrust of nature is so woven into modern Western cultural core values, that even some of those who describe themselves as agnostic, and not followers of any particular religion, hold parts of this indoctrination as absolute truth. So even when plants are talking to us, we are taught that it isn't real, or that we should not listen, because they cannot be trusted and might be channels for evil, or that what we hear cannot be true or trusted.

Epigenetics, which is a new area of genetic study that began to appear in textbooks during the last few years of my career as a textbook consultant and instructor in genetics, also teaches that DNA can record memories such as trauma, fear, love, safety, survival, and that those memories are passed forward to future generations.[24] How specific or complete that record can be is as yet unknown, but it stands to reason, given this information, that the trauma of the witch craze period still instills fear. Anyone having a deep connection with nature and natural healing, such as midwives, herbalists, healers, and members of indigenous cultures practicing any kind of shamanic healing, are seen as not to be trusted, and in the past were accused and executed as witches in front of their children, family, friends, and wider community. People today are fearful, and many don't even know why.

The classical Western medical profession was also on the rise during the latter part of the inquisition, and the accusations of Western doctors sent many to their deaths. Only doctors trained in a university were considered valid healers. All others –mostly women– were viewed as witches. During this time, many powerful plants with profound chemistry went from being viewed as medicine and keepers of knowledge, to tools of the devil crafted to mislead us.[25] Even as healers were being executed as witches for using these plants, doctors continued to study them for drug formulation. Once religion discarded secular' plant ointments as important and good, doctors tried to replicate them in a scientific

---

[24] Jane Maienschein, "Epigenesis and Preformationism," *The Stanford Encyclopedia of Philosophy*, (Spring 2017 Edition), https://plato.stanford.edu/archives/spr2017/entries/epigenesis/.

[25] Julia Semproniana Carreras, "De Metzineria Pirenaica," *Verdant Gnosis: Cultivating the Green Path Volume 4*, (Seattle: Revelore Press, 2018).

context,[26] which was acceptable because doctors were viewed as rational and immune to the influence of mother nature's wiles. Natural use of plants for healing became illegal. Nature is still viewed as evil and dangerous, and many of the great teacher plants with profound chemistry are still illegal.

Western culture still considers people who heal using the great teachers to be misguided at best, or crazy malevolent, and dangerous at worst. These beliefs are not only not shared by any shamanic culture that I am aware of, but the idea that nature has no value and is something that is only here for human use, is a very eco-unfriendly paradigm, and could very well bring about those "last days" stratified belief systems are so fond of using to scare followers into church approved behavioral patterns that strengthen and support existing stratified power systems.

Recognizing all these discussions and examples, in order to commune with nature, to perceive the wisdom of plants and animals, we must become fully conscious. We must give in and revel in the senses, in the sensuality of nature as a path transcendent. Enlightenment comes through the senses, and through learning to work with all the many senses of the body and being, not just the official five. Earth is our home and we are of the natural family of life here, part of Earth, and not separate. Studies of genetics have verified that all of life, all of its varied forms, are related and built of the same molecules as every other. Lucy Smith of the Dry Creek Pomo of California put it like this, "We all had to live together and get along with each other…I thought she was talking about us Indians and how we are supposed to get along. I found out later by my older sister that mother wasn't just talking about Indians, but the plants, animals, birds---everything on this Earth. They are our relatives and we better know how to act

---

[26] ibid.

around them."[27]

So, when I say that plants are sentient, what do I mean by that? The dictionary definition of sentience typically indicates that in order to be sentient, one must be able to perceive and feel things. One must be a creature that can suffer and feel pain such as humans and animals do. Furthermore, a sentient creature must possess the power to perceive, to reason, to think and to respond[28] As such, to be sentient means to experience pain, sensation, emotion, and to respond to varied stimuli.

Plants have been studied for these qualities and have been found capable of all of these criteria. Tomato plants can scream in pain at 220 khz,[29] which is just at the upper reach of human hearing, but they also produce much higher frequency sounds as well. Studies show "stressed plants emit airborne sounds that can be recorded remotely, both in acoustic chambers and in greenhouses. We recorded ~65 dBSPL ultrasonic sounds 10 cm from tomato and tobacco plants, implying that these sounds could be detected by some organisms from up to several meters away" and "We demonstrated for the first time that stressed plants emit remotely detectable sounds, similarly to many animals, using ultrasound clicks not audible to human ears. We also found that the sounds contain information, and can reveal plant state. The results suggest a new modality of signaling for plants and imply that other organisms could have evolved to hear, classify and respond to these sounds."[30] Tomato plants

---

[27] Malcolm Margolin, *The Way We Lived: California Indian Stories, Songs & Reminiscences*, (Heydey Books and the California Historical Society, 1993), 95.

[28] The Merriam-Webster Dictionary, s.v. "sentience (n.)," accessed January 22, 2020, https://www.merriam-webster.com/dictionary/sentien.

[29] Florianne Koechlin, "Tomatoes Talk, Birch Trees Learn – Do Plants Have Dignity?" January 2016, TEDxZurich video, https://youtu.be/i8YnvMpcrVI

[30] I. Khait, O. Lewin-Epstein, R. Sharon, K. Saban, R. Perelman, A. Boonman, Y.

can also produce over 200 responses to insect, animal, and human predators, only 20 of which are common to other plants.[31] Plants can identify a specific predator attacking them and respond specifically to that organism with chemistry that discourages the predation and communicates the threat to other plants around it so they can defend themselves as well. Trees definitely have consciousness. They have feelings, friends, family, memory, they feel pain, they sleep, they move, and are social beings.[32] Trees can count, recognize their own young from the offspring of others, help each other, and even share food with each other.[33] They can share information and perceived threats through their root system through the use of mycelial networking,[34] additionally, plants can communicate danger to their neighbors and the neighbor will close its stomata in response to the communication of a threat or danger.[35] Trees share info with their neighbors and indeed entire forests are communicating like a community does, and they can hear and respond to sound vibrations in various ways as well.

Yovel, L. Hadany "Plants Emit Informative Airborne Sounds Under Stress," *bioRxiv* 507590 (December 2019), https://doi.org/10.1101/507590

[31] ibid, 16.

[32] Greg Gage, "Electrical Experiments with Plants that Count and Communicate," TED video, (November 2017), https://www.ted.com/talksgreg_gage_electrical_experiments_with_plants_that_count_and_communicate?language=en.

[33] Peter Wohlleben, "The Hidden Life of Trees," YouTube video, (February 2016), https://youtu.be/1djibBPOfto.

[34] Suzanne Simard, "Wood Wide Web: The World of Trees Underneath the Surface," *New Statesman America* (August 2016), https://www.newstatesman.com/culture/nature/2016/08/wood-wide-web-world-trees-underneath-surface.

[35] Prof. Ariel Novoplansky, "Learning Plant Learning," TEDx Jaffa, (October 19, 2012),https://www.youtube.com/watch?v=aClSp71zfro.

Anthropologists have long wondered how traditional people know how to use plants so efficiently, especially highly toxic ones, with a minimum of poisoning accidents. When anthropologists ask shamans the world over how they know what plants to use in their healing work, how they know how to formulate them, and how they know a given plant or preparation of that plant is safe, they all answer in essentially the same way. They will say that it told them, or that the spirit of the plant came to them in a dream and instructed them. Indigenous people are able to communicate and commune with plants. Their cultures consider this behavior not only normal, but accurate and important. Talking to plants and spirits in these cultures is viewed as perfectly sane behavior. Non-western foraging cultures teach their members from a very young age that they can communicate with animals and plants and view it as an important part of a healthy, balanced relationship with nature. They are taught that plants and animals have souls and personalities, and that they want to interact with human consciousness, and have wisdom to share. These plants are viewed as capable of communication with us, and with each other.

A related but also stigmatized area of study is the use of entheogens by shamans to contact other consciousnesses in the forest. In order to thoroughly explore this topic, we must also look at studies of plants that contain profound chemistry, such as mind-altering substances, and the use of what we call "the great teachers" and how they are understood and viewed in Western and shamanic cultures. Since most of the Western world does not acknowledge this practice as valid experience or as true or stable behavior, plants, rocks, trees, and other natural beings are viewed as unconscious things. Fewer people hear them or connect with them and those that do are considered high or mentally ill. In response, those who are still able to perceive plant sentience, disconnect from the sentience of nature and are trained to be oblivious to its consciousness. In fact, Western culture actively enculturates people to believe that nature cannot communicate, is not conscious, and cannot instruct us. It teaches that talking to plants and animals is nothing more than lonely delusional behavior at best, and that plants and animals have no meaningful significance in the "real world." The result is that integration with the natural world becomes difficult to impossible for many as they grow to adulthood.

Interestingly, some very respected and educated individuals are seeking to reconnect with nature through the shaman guided use of entheogens. Entheogens are used nearly universally by westernized and traditional cultures. The difference is that entheogens are primarily used and viewed as medicine in traditional cultures and not for recreational use. I interviewed such a seeker in relation to his experiences with westernized use of LSD, and other entheogens in contrast with his medicinal experiences with entheogens with an experienced guide.

Paul is a Harvard and UC Berkeley educated IP and business attorney, business consultant, and international speaker, residing and practicing in San Francisco, California with education in anthropology in his foundational educational background. He has made ten journeys to Peru to engage ayahuasca in forty-nine ceremonies.[36] I found his observations and account of experiences to be very helpful in understanding the role of these kinds of plants in human healing and consciousness. He describes Ayahuasca as Papatua-head spirit-teacher.[37] He characterized ayahuasca as a bridge to the spirit world experience, like a language teacher. When you study a language with a teacher, you are taught how to communicate effectively as well as norms and values

---

[36] Paul Spiegel, Zoom Interview, Brita Wynn Dinsmore, (Conducted: February 2020).

[37] ibid.

that are part of that world. It teaches you how to communicate and relate in that world. I asked Paul if he thought people could communicate with the spirits of nature the same way without the use of this medicine. His response was very clarifying. He said that yes, he felt it was possible but that the effects of these plants change you and stay with you for a long time, maybe permanently, and so change the way you see the world overall. He said that it was like coming into the experience as a person who has always worn sunglasses, all the time, everywhere and then someone took them gently from you and said "you won't need these anymore" and suddenly really being able to experience true vision.[38]

Paul's many ayahuasca journeys, he believes but was unaware of in the moment, were a type of training that later helped prepare him for an interaction with the very toxic Yew tree, whose spirit he calls, "Mamataxa," during cancer treatment using a chemotherapy drug, docetaxel, that comes from this tree. He believes conscious work with "Mamataxa" during this process ultimately saved his life. He was able to seek her out and talk with her directly and ask for her help in killing his cancer, which she agreed to do.[39] So through his work with ayahuasca, ceremonially engaged, and guided by experienced shaman, he was able to transcend the westernized enculturated blindness to plant consciousness and not only communicate with plants but ask for, and receive, actual healing of his physical body with far fewer ill side effects than are usual for this particular chemotherapy drug.

We learn how to perceive our world through the lens of culture. This enculturative process can effectively blind us to other possibilities of true reality because we believe so strongly that the reality culture teaches us is the one true

---

[38] ibid.

[39] Paul Spiegel, "Paul A. Spiegel: A Shamanic Nexus for Cancer Treatment," BIL Talks, LA (September 2016), https://www.youtube.com/watch?v=Mrgy3DhY70k.

reality. We are taught not to trust intuition, not to trust our senses beyond the limits of those teachings, and not to believe anything not validated by scientific method. There is, however, quite a lot of science that validates plant consciousness and sentience. This concept is inconvenient while we are still harvesting forests at unsustainable rates.

Moving forward, we should make it a priority to determine exactly what kind of consciousness trees and plants have. Consider as you go about your life how plants communicate with us and with each other. How can we train ourselves to be more aware of the consciousness of nature? What tools can we develop to help us transcend our cultural perceptual limitations? The first step is to unravel the cultural conditioning that teaches that plants are unconscious and not sentient beings, and then simply to hold space that it is possible. To study how indigenous cultures communicate with plants and engage them as equals and allies. This can be a powerful direction that we as Westerners can embrace as we move into a more conscious future.

On The Quintessence of Herbs and Methods to Obtain it

Robert Allen Bartlett

"Now I will teach and describe the secret of the Arts, which secret is at the heart of all secrets hidden in the art of Alchemy... For I shall here teach you to know the spirits of herbs, trees, and all growing things; how to separate them from their bodies, and also how to purify the four elements and restore them to their First Being and their perfect power; that is, that when the elements are purified, how they can be put together again and make a perfect and fixed body of them, which is then glorified and has a miraculous effect" [1]

The words of 15th century alchemist Isaac Holland in his 'Opera Vegetabilis', wherein he describes the medicinal preparation of plants from the uniquely alchemical perspective. Holland gives a clear description of preparing what he calls the 'Quintessence' of the vegetable realm having medicinal benefits bordering the miraculous. A hundred years earlier, the Catalonian monk and alchemist known as John of Rupecissa, with the horrors of past plagues in mind, urged his fellow alchemists, physicians, and philosophers to find a universal panacea that could cure all diseases that affect

---

[1] Isaac Holland, *A Compendium of Writings by Johan Isaac Hollandus,* Edited by A.E. Waite (University Books: NY 1967), 11.

mankind in preparation for the apocalyptic coming of the Antichrist. He believed he had found this medicine in a specially prepared spirit of wine, which he called the 'Quintessence' or 'Mortal Heaven' boasting a similar miraculous effect.

> *'...philosophers, and many others, have sought this One Thing with great labor, and have found that which preserves the human body from corruption, and prolongs life, conducts itself, with respect to other elements, as it were like the Heavens; from which they understood that the Heavens are a substance above the Four Elements. And just as the Heavens, with respect to the other elements, are held to be the fifth substance (for they are indestructible, stable, and suffer no foreign admixture), so also this One Thing (compared to the forces of our body) is an indestructible essence, drying up all the superfluities of our bodies, and has been philosophically called by the above-mentioned name. It is neither hot and dry like fire, nor cold and moist like water, nor warm and moist like air, nor dry and cold like earth. But it is a skillful, perfect equation of all the Elements, a right commingling of natural forces, a most particular union of spiritual virtues, an indissoluble uniting of body and soul. It is the purest and noblest substance of an indestructible body, which cannot be destroyed nor harmed by the Elements, and is produced by Art.'*[2]

To understand these concepts in the sense that when they were written, we need to go further back in time, about two thousand years to be exact. As the Egyptian and Greek cultures merged, there arose a philosophy about nature and

[2] Benedictus Figulus, *A Golden and Blessed Casket of Nature's Marvels* (James Elliot and Co.:London 1893), 8.

reality which would prevail until the 18th century and indeed still prevails in certain areas of the world.

Around 500BCE, the Greek philosophers were in agreement with physician/philosopher Empedocles that the natural world consisted of four basic elements, fire, air, water, and earth blended into a myriad of forms. That last word, 'Forms', is a loaded word itself in ancient cosmology and the first word we need to describe.

In the ancient cosmological model, there were three realms or worlds. The Intellectual World, as the highest and most sublime realm, is where it all begins. This is the realm of mind and of archetypes, the place where 'Ideas' or 'Forms' originate. The Form is the complete blueprint of a thing not just how it looks, but what it's made of, how it's made, why it is made, even its ultimate end. The Form is the active, motive force of a thing, but without something to act on, it is purely potential. What Form does act on is a certain undefinable something which is distributed everywhere and possesses all known properties in potential but none actual, so it can't really be described and in a sense doesn't even exist. This invisible 'something' had to be given a name and it was called 'Materia Prima' the first matter or just Matter. Having the potential to take on any property and yet exhibiting no properties on its own, Matter was seen as the perfect medium into which Forms were seeded. The primary qualities or properties of hot, cold, wet, and dry which were potential in Matter are now moved by the Form to become actual.

The primary qualities combine to generate the four elements, fire, air, water, and earth in the proper proportions and arrangement as called for by the Form and it manifests here in the Elementary World also called the 'Sublunary World'. Between the Intellectual Realm and our Elementary Realm, lay the Celestial Realm, home to the stars and planets which influence the affairs of our world. Also known as Heaven, this realm is composed of the most subtle, incorruptible, immortal and intelligent substance, the Fifth Element. That is why the stars and planets are so permanent compared to the constant ebb and flow of Elemental force here in the ever-changing Elementary Realm.

And that is the challenge in medicine, through diet and drugs, to keep on top of this constant change of corruptible elemental forces within the body in order to maintain our particular balance of the elements. 'Aristotle says that every Form of every nature, animal, vegetable, and mineral, is produced by the power of Matter, intrinsically, except the human soul, which, being of a different and higher nature than matter, is given, extrinsically, by the Prime Mover.

But since two different things cannot be mixed or joined into one, the soul being a certain divine light and substance, emanating immortal from divine springs and on the other hand, the body is wholly earthly material having its origin in gross, rank, elementary matter, mortal of itself, unfit for motion and therefore far inferior to the soul; wherefore it can never be united to the soul, so different from itself, except through a third, a Medium participating in the nature of each a quasi-body and quasi-soul, by which the soul may be added and joined to the body.

Such a medium they suppose it to be, the Spirit or Soul of the World, i.e., what we call Fifth Essence, because it consists not of the four elements, but is a certain fifth one, above and beside them. This Spirit is of the same form in the Greater World as in the Lesser, i.e., the human body, our Spirit, which arises from the former, and is with it one and the same Spirit. Through this medium, the soul descends and is poured into the heart, which is in the center of the Lesser World (human body), and from thence is diffused through all the parts and members of its body.'[3]

---

[3] Figulus, 13-14.

> *The ancients gave the name of Body to whatever is fixed and resists the action of fire; moreover, it has the power of retaining in a compound that is essentially incorporeal and volatile, and attempts to volatilize the Body i.e., the Soul.*
>
> *Spirit they called that which constitutes the bond between Body and Soul, and, by abiding with the Body, compels the Soul to return to it. And yet, Body, Soul, and Spirit are not three things, but three different aspects of the same thing.' The Body perfects and retains the Soul, and imparts real being to it and the whole work, while the Soul manifests its power in this body, and all this is accomplished through the mediation of the Spirit.'*[4]

'Some term it Spirit of the World, others Celestial Fire, others again Vital Spirit, Natural Heat, or Innate Heat, by which nothing else is denoted than that oft mentioned Spirit of things Celestial and Inferior, the Gluten of Body and Soul. On examining the thing more fully, this is simply the heat and humor of Sun and Moon, administrators of Heaven. The Sun is Lord of all Virtues of the elements and the Moon, by virtue of the Sun, is the Mistress of Generation, of increase and decrease. Whatever good we possess is from the Sun whence Heraclitus deservedly calls it the Fount of Heavenly Light.

From these two founts (Sun and Moon) arise that mundane, natural, and vital Spirit, permeating all things, giving life to all things and consistence, binding, moving, and filling all things, immense renewal in Nature's charge, through whom, as mediator, every hidden property, every virtue, all life is propagated in inferior bodies, in herbs, in metals, in stones, in things inanimate, so that in the whole world, there is nothing wanting in a spark of this spirit.

---

[4] Peter Bonus, *A New Pearl of Great Price* (James Elliot & Co., London 1894), 261-262.

Therefore, this Spirit, when whole and undiminished in our bodies, and not impeded by things extraneous, is Our Natural Heat, by which everything is digested for the sustenance and multiplying of individuals. The said Spirit and Natural Heat, must be increased and comforted so that it may better and more strongly perform its functions. But as agents act not with inferiors but with equals, so must also this comforting take place through the Spirits equal, viz., through the Celestial Heat of the Sun and Moon and other planets, or with those things in which the virtue of Sun and Moon are most potent, abundant, and least bound up with matter.

Seek then, that Celestial Heat of the Sun and Moon, dwelling in a more incorruptible substance, under the Moons intermittent orb, and make this similar to our heat and spirit; so that prepared as medicine and sweet food, when taken into the mouth it may immediately penetrate the human frame, greatly holding to itself every fleshy thing, increasing, restoring and nourishing the incorrupt virtue and Spirit of Life, digesting the crude and undigested, removing the superfluous, making natural water abound, and augmenting, comforting and inflaming the Natural Heat or Fire.[55]

'But some may affirm that such a medicine cannot be found in the whole sphere of this nether world, because all things created, being either elements or composed and congenital with them, are therefore corruptible, and hence that this medicine and incorruptible root of life can nowhere be found.

Figulus instructs that we must look more deeply into the Book of Nature in order to discover that 'there is in the elements something besides corruptible qualities, for the elements and their compounds, in addition to crass matter, are composed of a subtle substance or intrinsic Radical Humidity, diffused through their elemental parts, simple and wholly

[5] Figulus, 14, 16.

incorruptible, long preserving the things themselves in vigor.

Called the Spirit of the World, it proceeds from the Soul of the World. This Spirit by its virtue fecundates all subjects natural and artificial, pouring into them those hidden properties that we call the Fifth Essence or Quintessence. This Fifth Essence was created by the Almighty for the preservation of the four elements of the human body, even as Heaven (Celestial Realm) is for the preservation of the universe. Therefore, is this Fifth Essence a spiritual medicine, which is of Nature and the Heart of Heaven (and never of a mortal and corrupt quality), that makes life possible; it is the Fount of Medicine, the preservation of life, the restoration of health, and in this may be the cherished renewal of lost youth and serene health be found.[6]

> *This spiritual Light, which we call Nature or Soul of the World, is a spiritual body which may be rendered visible and tangible by alchemical processes; but as it is naturally invisible it is called Spirit. It is a living universal fluid, diffused throughout Nature, and which penetrates everything. It is the most subtle of all substances; the most powerful, by reason of its inherent qualities; it penetrates every Body and determines the Forms in which it displays its activity. By its action it frees the Forms from all imperfection; it makes the impure pure, the imperfect perfect, the mortal immortal, by its indwelling. This essence or Spirit emanated from the beginning from the Center and incorporated itself with the substance of which the universe is formed. It is the "Salt of the Earth," and without its presence the plant would not grow, nor the field become green and the more this essence is condensed, concentrated, and coagulated in the Forms the more stable they become. It is the most subtle of all substances; incorruptible and immoveable in its*

[6] Figulus.

> *essence, it fills the infinities of space. The sun and planets are but coagulations of this universal principle; from their beating heart they distribute the abundance of their life and send it forth into the Forms of the inferior world, and into all creatures acting about their own centre and raising the Forms on the way of perfection. The Forms in which this living principle establishes itself become perfect and durable so that they no longer decay nor deteriorate nor change in contact with the air; water can no longer dissolve them, nor fire destroy them, nor the terrestrial elements devour them.*[7]

This Spirit is obtained in the same way as it is communicated to the earth by the stars; and this is performed by means of the Water, which serves as a vehicle to it. It is not the Philosopher's Stone but this may be prepared from it by fixing the volatile.'[8]

In his 'Archidoxis', Paracelsus writes, "The Quintessence, then, is a certain matter extracted from all things which Nature has produced, and from everything which has life corporeally in itself, a matter most subtly purged of all impurities and mortality, and separated from all the elements." From this it is evident that the Quintessence is, so to say, a nature, a force, a virtue, and a medicine, once, indeed, shut up within things, but now free from any domicile and from all outward incorporation. And now we must see by what method the Quintessence is to be extracted. There are many ways indeed: some by addition, as the spirit of wine; others by balsamites; some by separation of the elements, and many other processes which we do not here particularize.'

---

[7] Trithemius, *Confession of Trithemius,* From *Traite Des Causes Secondes*, Trans. A.A. Wells, 2

[8] Figulus.

'But by whatsoever method it takes place, the Quintessence should not be extracted by the mixture or the addition of incongruous matters; but the element of the Quintessence must be extracted from a separated Body, and in like manner, by that separated body which is extracted. Different methods are found by which the Quintessence may be extracted, for instance, by sublimation, by calcination, by strong waters, by corrosives, by sweet things, by sour and so on, in whatever way it may be possible. And here this is to be taken care of, that everything which shall have been mixed with the Quintessence by the necessity of extraction, must again be drawn off from it, so that the Quintessence may remain alone, unpolluted, and unmixed with any other things'.[9]

Most alchemical preparations begin with the controlled death and putrefaction of the subject matter, this is called the 'Nigredo' stage because everything turns dark and foul

[9] Paracelsus, 25.

smelling. This fermentation stage can be an actual fermentation process, like making wine, or it can be a digestion of a prepared medium such as alcohol with the subject. It can also take the form of a distillation of fresh material, slowly raising the temperature until nothing more will distill over and all that's left is a black lump of charcoal. Things don't give up the ghost until they die, but instead of allowing the volatile Soul/Spirit to escape, it is trapped within the 'glass coffin' and fermented liquid, separated from its Body.

After this separation of Body and Soul/Spirit, the isolation and purification begin. This is the 'Albedo' stage of the work, the 'whitening', as the separated parts are purified thus becoming lighter, brighter and more subtle. In the final stage, called 'Rubedo', the 'reddening', the purified Body, Soul, and Spirit of the matter are reunited and, in a sense, reborn in a 'glorified' form concentrated with the Fifth Essence, the Quintessence in our original matter.

The methods to accomplish all of this are legion, especially in the vegetable realm once you understand the principles. The following two examples taken from that master of medicine and alchemy, Paracelsus, serve to illustrate:

> *Those things are called growing in this place which fall and grow again, as herbs, leaves, and the like. For extracting the Quintessence of these, several methods have been found out by the addition of other things. But they should be extracted without admixture of anything, so that they may retain their taste, color, and odor; and that these properties may be increased in them, not diminished.'*
>
> *Take fresh growing things, bruised as completely as possible. Put them in some fitting vessel, and set this in a venter equinus (warm digestive heat, about 100 degrees F) for four weeks. Afterwards distill them by means of a waterbath.*

Collect all of the distillate that will come over with the heat of the bath.

Dry the remaining residue, grind it finely and return it to the distillation vessel along with the collected distillate. Digest again for eight days, and once more distill by the waterbath.

Thus the Quintessence will ascend by the alembic, but the Body will remain at the bottom. Then take at length this distilled water, add it again to this fresh growing thing, and so, by means of a pelican (refluxing apparatus) let them be digested together six days. Separate the liquid from the solids by pressing and filtration. Digest the liquid for four days and separate any solids that may have settled out by decanting the liquid off. In this way you will have it perfect in odor, in juiciness, in taste, and in virtues, as well as consisting of a thick substance.

We will now teach the method of extracting the Quintessence from aromatic spices such as frankincense, myrrh, camphor and the like. First the Quintessence ought to be reduced to another form, and at length, to be separated therefrom.

Take oil of almonds, with which let an aromatic body be mixed, and let them be digested together in a glass vessel in the Sun, for the proper time, until they are reduced to a paste. Afterwards let them be pressed out from their dregs. In this way the Body is separated from the Quintessence, which is thus mixed with the oil, from which it is separated in the following way:

Take rectified ardent wine (190 proof) into which let the aforesaid oil be poured, and let them be left in the process of digestion for six days. Afterwards let this wine be distilled in an ashbath. The ardent wine will ascend, and the Quintessence with it. The oil will remain at the bottom without any of the Quintessence remaining. Afterwards let

> *this wine be distilled by the waterbath, and the Quintessence will remain at the bottom in the form of an oil distinct from all similar ones.'* [10]

Another method, if you have access to a large supply of the chosen herb, is to steam distill out its essential oil from one portion, set another portion to ferment and later distill out the volatile Spirit. Dry, incinerate, and calcine a third portion to obtain a light grey to white ash. Pour distilled water over the ash in order to dissolve the salt hidden in the bulk of the ash. Filter off this water into a dish and let it dry, whereupon you will find a white crystalline solid. Place the dish of crystals out in the night air, protected from rain and dust, until they liquefy. Collect as much of this liquefied salt as possible then allow it to dry very gently. This now purified Body is our Luna, or Philosophical Moon.

The volatile Spirit and Essential Oil collected earlier can be poured together, creating a golden essence, which is our Philosophical Sun. Our Sun and Moon are now united and digested into a clear golden liquid, our Quintessence.

Figulus provides a universal guide for extraction of the Quintessence in just a few sentences:

> *"To extract the Quintessence of plants and animal substances, they must be dissolved into their Three Principles. Pour the Water on its own Salt dropwise until dissolved and the Oil has penetrated the Body. Separate any undissolved Feces then the pure liquid is set on a graduated fire.*
>
> *The volatile Spirit will also make the fixed volatile, and the fixed will make the volatile stable. Then the Magistery is finished and the medicinal species are transformed into an Arcanum and Quintessence which will accomplish miracles*

---

[10] Paracelsus, 33-34.

in all diseases.

We do not say that medicine is quite as incorruptible as Heaven, but being generated from matter above all others and incorruptible with respect to them, and simply formed by the separation therefrom of all corruptible elements, it could be kept, if necessary, 10,000 years.

For the more Form a thing has, the more entity, virtue, and operation it has. Those things in which the Idea (which is the Form) is least merged into the Body, or Matter, have the most potent virtues, because being the most Formal (Spiritual), they can with very little Matter effect very much."[11]

'Just as the very smallest quantity of saffron tinges a vast body of water, yet the whole of it is not saffron. Thus in like manner, must it be laid down with regard to the Quintessence, that its quantity is small in woods, in herbs, in stones, and other similar things.'

We cannot speak of the grades in the same way as grades are applied to simples in medicine (Note: such as saffron being hot in the second degree and dry in the first degree), for this reason that there is no possible comparison between the grades of a Quintessence and the grades of simples, nor ought the comparison be attempted; but when such gradation is made it is found that the excellence and virtue of one is greater than of another, but not the complexion. For whatever be the property in a simple form, such is the property of their Quintessence, not more sluggish, but much stronger and more excellent.[12]

'Now the fact that the Quintessence cures all diseases does not arise from temperature (heating or cooling), but from

[11] Figulus.

[12] Paracelsus, 23, 26.

an innate property, namely, it's great cleanliness and purity, by which, after a wonderful manner, it alters the body into its own purity, and entirely changes it. When, therefore, the Quintessence is separated from that which is not the Quintessence, as the Soul from its Body, and itself taken into the Body, what infirmity is able to withstand this so noble, pure, and powerful nature, or to take away our life?'[13]

'Although we have put forth lofty and numerous virtues of the Quintessence, nevertheless, only the smallest part of their forces and qualities has been told. But we have principally made it clear how these things are to be understood; yet least of all have we been able to tell what and how great are their powers and virtues. From this may be hinted how great is the power which we have in our hands, only let us know how to use it well.'[14]

In a comment made by the physician Dr. Theodor Kerkring, who, in his 1678 translation and commentary to Basil Valentine's, 'Triumphal Chariot of Antimony', describes the medicinal activity of these preparations and cautions us to perform a general purge and cleansing of the body prior to using the alchemical remedy in order to elicit its maximum effect and although he is speaking about the metallic medicines he is writing about, his comment applies in general to all alchemical medicines; he writes:

"These Medicaments, which perform their operations, not by sensible forces, as cathartics, emetics, diaphoretics, and the like are wont to operate, but insensibly uniting their own more pure Universal Spirit unto our Spirits, amend Nature and restore health, are not to be used, unless where the Body hath first been cleansed from the impurities of pecant humors, otherwise you cast pearls into a dunghill, where (overwhelmed with filths) they cannot shine and

---

[13] Paracelsus, 23.

[14] ibid, 36.

manifest their virtues."[15]

I have allowed the alchemists to speak for themselves on these matters. The processes described and many other related spagyric methods do indeed work to produce powerful medicinal agents. This is evident today by the growing interest in spagyric medicine and alchemy. And as to the miraculous effects ascribed to these medicines by ancient practitioners, they do seem to go above and beyond the range of listed healing properties; where, for example, a simple calming herb cures a years old knee injury in just a few days. The addition of the salts into the plant extract is a signature operation of herbal spagyrics and this single step is very transforming to the substance.

The saline qualities of the final spagyric extract allow the material to be absorbed more completely and without destructive metabolism by the body. Some attribute this to a shift in the oxidation-reduction properties of the extract such that the body recognizes the material as already broken down and ready for assimilation thus preserving more of the healing properties which might have been lost as the body metabolized the medicine prior to absorption. There is research underway today by a group that suspects the spagyric medicines contain a type of exotic matter unknown to modern science. The idea that the quintessence streams down upon us daily from the Sun and stars and becomes incorporated into materials which are then spagyrically prepared to concentrate this quintessence, forms the basis of their research into the quantum world. The quintessence is said to conduct intelligence and so the result would be programmable matter. And maybe that is the real key to all of this that the spagyrically prepared medicines bring in an

---

[15] Basil Valentine, *Triumphal Chariot of Antimony.*

intelligence that can direct the body's self-healing processes more efficiently.

I hope the interest and implementation of spagyric medicine continues because, as more research is done, it all seems to vindicate the ancient alchemist's claims of 'miraculous cures' and from this the possibility of long and healthy lives attuned to Nature opens for everyone.

Contributors

PAUL BEYERL has been known as an educator in the field of botanical medicine as well as Herbal Magick since the 1970s. His book '*The Master Book of Herbalism*', published in 1984 is selling as strong as ever today. When his seminal book '*A Compendium of Herbal Magick*' was published in 1996 he had documented information on 330 species. Data he gathered for this book had to meet his requirement of being academically sound with documented historical accuracy. Today his research has files on approximately 2,500 different species which are used in folk magic, religious ceremony and shamanic practices. His research (now aprox 75% complete) has taken him through research from the subcontinent (primarily India and Nepal), the southern third of Africa, North America and Europe.

He is the founder of *The Rowan Tree Church* (incorporated in 1980) with its Mystery School for advanced training in Magick and the Mysteries. His work includes *The Hermit's Grove* which is the imprint as a publishing house as well as the umbrella for the botanical programs including '*The Master Herbalist Program*' and the new botanical gardens.

With his partner, Rev. Gerry, the Beyerl's have relocated the Church and Grove's Administrative and Publishing to a new Retreat Center they are establishing in the hills of the Root River near Houston, Minnesota in the Driftless Area of the Upper Mississippi, untouched by the drift of the last two glacial periods.

BRANDON WESTON is a healer, writer, and folklorist living in the Arkansas Ozarks. He is author of Ozark Folk Magic: Plants, Prayers, and Healing and owner of Ozark Healing Traditions, a collective of articles, lectures, and workshops focusing on traditions of medicine, magic, and folklore from the Ozark Mountain region. As an active healer, his work with clients includes everything from spiritual cleanses to house blessings and all the weird and wonderful ailments in between. He comes from a long line of Ozark hillfolk and works hard to keep the traditions that he's collected alive and true for generations to come.

PROFESSOR CHARLES PORTERFIELD is an old-fashioned, no-nonsense, Old Testament reader and rootworker. He is the co-author of Hoodoo Bible Magic, the author of A Deck of Spells and The Sporting Life, and has been published in Volume 5 of the Verdant Gnosis. A well-known cartomancer, he regularly lectures and teaches on cartomancy, cartomantic methods, hoodoo, and conjure to help preserve and pass on the roots of the work as well as consults, prescribes, and divines work for those in need. He currently lives in Denton, Texas with his wife, children, and grandchildren.

RICHARD SPELKER is an independent researcher who has been researching the history of artist materials for over 25 years. He has collected over 1000 historical writing ink recipes including many for magical inks. He has given many ink making classes over the years, such as the San Francisco Friends of Calligraphy, The San Francisco Center for the Book and the National Paper and Book Intensive. He has a BFA from the University of Minnesota in studio arts and art history.

GIULIA TUROLLA is an Italian witch, High Priestess and teacher in the Temple of Ara tradition (Tempio di Ara, in Italy). She graduated with honors in Archaeology and Ancient World Cultures from Alma Mater Studiorum –University of Bologna and her field of specialization is ancient magical/religious technology and culture. She has been leading circles for the Temple of Ara since 2008 and actively teaching study groups and advanced workshops since 2012. As an artisan, she also creates shamanic and magical tools focused on European magical traditions. Some of her work may be found at Bosco di ArtemesiA.

JESSE HATHAWAY DIAZ is a folklorist, artist and performer living in New York City. With initiations in several forms of witchcraft from Europe and the Americas, he is also a lifelong student of Mexican curanderismo, a root worker and card reader, an initiated olosha in Lucumí, and a Tatá Quimbanda. For the last decade he has been a member of Theatre Group Dzieci, an experimental ensemble based in NY dedicated to the search for the sacred through the medium of theatre. He is half of www.wolf-and-goat.com, a store specializing in occult art, esoterica and *materia magica* from many traditions including Traditional Craft and Quimbanda.

BRITA WYNN DINSMORE holds a four-field M.A. in Anthropology with an in-depth emphasis in Cultural Ethnobotany and Native American culture as well as genetics, archaeology and ethnography. She recently retired from 25 years as a college professor to create and open The Queen's Ranch and Cronewytch's Cauldron Herb Farm and Learning Center in Shelton, Washington. She has 25 years of experience teaching anthropology and herbalism as well as 20 years teaching herbal apprentice course work and currently teaches course work that includes the Gaia Conscious Herbal Apprenticeship Medicine Path, medicine making workshops, aromatherapy, and traditional herbal folk magic as well as studies of what she calls "the great green teachers," which are plants like belladonna, henbane and aconite. She also has extensive experience with wortcunning, esoteric herbalism and herbal shamanism.

ROBERT ALLEN BARTLETT is a world-renowned lab alchemist who teaches Alchemy at Spagyricus Institute located in Snohomish, WA. He is student of Frater Albertus and chief chemist at Paracelsus Laboratories. He also produces a line of spagyric and homeopathic cell salts under the Terra Vitae label. Bartlett has authored the books, *Real Alchemy: A Primer of Practical Alchemy, The Way of the Crucible and The Temper of Herbs*. He lectures and gives classes around the world and is an Adept member of the International Alchemy Guild, preserving Alchemical Knowledge since the sixteenth century.

ARTISTS

CASANDRA JOHNS is a designer, illustrator, and herbalist residing in the Pacific Northwest. She works with independent publishers like Autonomous Press, Combustion Books, Minor Compositions, and AK Press, and with PUSH Collective, a worker-owned design group. Find more of her work at www.houseofhands.net

EDITORS

MARCUS MCCOY is the originator of the bioregional animist practice, author of the original bioregional animism blog, and co-founder of the Viridis Genii Symposium. He holds a BA in transpersonal anthropology in the study of the world's magical and spiritual systems. Marcus is an esoteric herbalist, metal artist, distiller, perfumer, and blacksmith. His metal work focuses on combining traditional folk magic with alchemical practices combining the realms of mineralia, vegetalia, and animalia into potent magical items though his work at Troll Cunning Forge.

CATAMARA ROSARIUM is a master herbalist, ritual artist, botanical alchemist, and proprietor of Rosarium Blends. Her extensive herbal experience is motivated by a deep attraction to plants, scents, and their impact on the senses. She has undertaken numerous unique esoteric and herbal training programs that have influenced her work, along with the spirit world and the gnosis of green wood. Catamara is the co-founder and convener of the Viridis Genii Symposium and Viridis Press. She has previously appeared in Sorita D'Este's Hekate anthology,*Her Sacred Fires* (2010), *Clavis* 4, and *Verdant Gnosis*, Vol. 1. More information on her herbal work can be found on the Rosarium Blends website: rosariumblends.com.

KIM SCHWENK, MLIS is a rare book cataloger at UC San Diego, Special Collections & Archives Library and an antiquarian bookseller with Lux Mentis, Booksellers. She has a specialization in American and European witchcraft history, history of early printed occult texts, and bibliographic studies of early magical curses using plants and objects. She also is active in occult sciences and the occult book community both as a researcher and a practitioner. Currently, she is researching "occult ex libris," otherwise known as "hex libris" or occult bookplates.

CPSIA information can be obtained
at www.ICGtesting.com
Printed in the USA
LVHW010125290621
691364LV00008B/49